DEALING WITH SCHOOL BULLYING

Society's educational Disgrace!

ROBERTA CAVA

Copyright © 2013 by Roberta Cava

This book is licensed for your personal enjoyment only and may not be re-sold or given away to other people. If you would like to share this book with another person, please purchase an additional copy for each recipient. If you're reading this book and did not purchase it, or it was not purchased for your use only, then please purchase your own copy. Thank you for respecting the hard work of this author.

Dealing with School Bullying
- Society's educational disgrace!
Roberta Cava

Published by Cava Consulting

info@dealingwithdifficultpeople.info

Discover other titles by Roberta Cava at
www.dealingwithdifficultpeople.info

National Library of Australia
Cataloguing-in-publication data:

ISBN 978-0-9923402-1-6

BOOKS BY ROBERTA CAVA

Non-Fiction

Dealing with Difficult People (23 publishers – in 17 languages)
Dealing with Difficult Situations – at Work and at Home
Dealing with Difficult Spouses and Children
Dealing with Difficult Relatives and In-Laws
Dealing with Domestic Violence and Child Abuse
Dealing with School Bullying
Dealing with Workplace Bullying
Retirement Village Bullies
Keeping Our Children Safe
Just say no
What am I going to do with the rest of my life?
Before tying the knot – Questions couples Must ask each other Before they marry!
How Women can advance in business
Survival Skills for Supervisors and Managers
Human Resources at its Best!
Human Resources Policies and Procedures - Australia
Employee Handbook
Easy Come – Hard to go – The Art of Hiring, Disciplining and Firing Employees
Time and Stress – Today's silent killers
Take Command of your Future – Make things Happen
Belly Laughs for All! – Volumes 1 to 6
Wisdom of the World! The happy, sad and wise things in life!

Fiction

That Something Special
Something Missing
Trilogy: Life Gets Complicated
Life Goes On
Life Gets Better

ACKNOWLEDGEMENTS

Special thanks to Tim Field (of website *'Bully OnLine'* in the UK) for his valuable contributions. Many thanks to the victims of school violence who took the time to tell their horror stories about the abuse they had either observed or as a victim.

Many thanks to Doreen Orion, MD, *'I Know You Really Love Me;'* David Kinchin *'Post Traumatic Stress Disorder: The Invisible Injury;'* Dr. Stanton E. Samenow, *'Straight Talk about Criminals'* and *'Inside the Criminal Mind;'* Edmonton Police Services and Constable Rick Cole *'School Resource Officer Program;'* Citizens Against Bullying Association of Northern Alberta (CABA); Bully B'Ware *'Take Action Against Bullying;'* Professor Peter Smith, Goldsmith's College University of London *'Bullying - Don't Suffer in Silence;'* Ted Brierley of Victorian Association of State Secondary Principals *'Guidelines on Countering Bullying Behaviour in Primary and Post-Primary Schools, September 1993;'* Ken Rigby, University of Southern Australia; VicHealth *'Together we do better'* Campaign; Restorative Justice; Maroochydore School High School *'Process for Dealing with Issues Related to Bullying;'* Centre for Adolescent Health *'Gatehouse Project;'* Department of Education Employment and Training Victoria *'Student Code of Conduct;'* The Alannah & Madeline Foundation *'Buddy Bears Schools Program;'* Get Your Angries Out Web page; Department of Education & The Arts, Victoria, *'Bullying. No Way!'* New Zealand Police *'New Zealand Stop Bullying Guidelines for Schools;'* Rod Lumper and Vereniging voor Openbaar Onderwijs *for 'Netherlands - Bullying at School: How to deal with it'* for giving me permission to use their information in this book.

Memorial to Tim Field:

Tim Field died on January 15, 2006 at the age of 53 from cancer. He was a world authority on bullying and psychiatric injury, and author of the best-selling **Bully in Sight** (1997). His vision was to attain a bully-free world, and he campaigned in schools, further and higher education, and the workplace to achieve this.

He lectured all over the world and worked personally on more than 5,000 bullying cases, highlighting the lack of understanding for victims. He revealed patterns showing how trade unions often failed to deal effectively with the problem among their members.

Field believed that bullying was the single most important social issue today. His work inspired and influenced international anti-bullying organisations, while his personal energy, commitment and knowledge restored sanity and saved lives. The world misses this dedicated anti-bullying campaigner.

Dealing with School Bullying – Australia's Educational Disgrace!

Table of Contents

Introduction	1
Chapter 1 - What is Bullying?	3
Chapter 2 - Health Disorders related to School Bullying	15
Chapter 3 - Bullying at School	25
Chapter 4 - Case Studies – Australia	45
Chapter 5 - Case Studies - United Kingdom	53
Chapter 6 - Case Studies – Canada	67
Chapter 7 - Case Studies - United States	83
Chapter 8 - Case Studies - Japan and Germany	99
Chapter 9 - How to Prevent and Stop School Bullying	101
Chapter 10 - How to Prevent and Stop School Bullying - Australia and New Zealand	105
Chapter 11 - How to Prevent and Stop School Bullying - United Kingdom	151
Chapter 12 - How to Prevent and Stop School Bullying - United States, Canada and The Netherlands	163
Conclusion	193
Bibliography	195
Web Connections	199

INTRODUCTION

Abuse of any kind is abhorrent to everyone except the bullies that use it. Bullying behaviour, often, starts in the home. There's a lot of anecdotal evidence to suggest that people who are bullies as adults were bullies at home and at school and learned they could get away with it.

Children watch how their parents and siblings settle disputes. Children copy what they see - and if they see their role models settling disputes with violence, they will copy that behaviour. They will likely bully siblings, friends, those in day-care facilities and ultimately at school. If conflicts at home are settled by negotiation and discussion, children learn to use their heads instead of their fists or bullying behaviour to deal with difficult situations. However, if the parents (their role models) deal with disputes by having shouting matches or use aggressive behaviour - their children are likely to clone this behaviour.

If this unacceptable behaviour is not stopped - it will naturally go with the child into our schools. Do all children from such homes become bullies - of course not, but the apple seldom falls far from the tree. Under most circumstances, the bullying child will have bullying parents.

And then there's the school system. Slowly, but surely government bodies have taken the control away from teachers and administrators. These teachers are forced to teach at the level of the lowest common denominator in their classes and spend much of their valuable time trying to re-channel the energies of their hyperactive or bullying students. There are too many students per teacher, so teachers spend less time with each child. School curriculum puts heavy emphasis on knowledge and little on how to work co-operatively with others. Also, sometimes teachers and schools find it easier to *'look the other way'* when faced with a bullying episode.

This book stresses that if we don't start at the beginning (in the home) the problem will not change. Unless we stop bullying in our schools and give teachers more authority to deal with these bullies - the message will remain that bullying behaviour (although not condoned) is allowed.

These bullying cowards know of no other way to live life except to overpower others. Until legal zero-tolerance school bullying laws are enforced, children will not be properly protected from the bullying behaviour that seems to permeate our schools.

Chapter 1

WHAT IS BULLYING?

Although this book is about school bullying, it's important to know the different kinds of abuse, because bullies are often abusive in many areas of their lives.

Bullying is a pattern of constant, daily fault-finding, criticism, segregation, exclusion and undermining that occurs for weeks or months. Each incident can be trivial, and on their own do not represent an offence or grounds for disciplinary action. The average bullying episode is brief, approximately 37 seconds long, but emotional scars from bullying can last a lifetime. Recovery from a bullying experience can take between two to five years, and some people never fully recover. Bullying differs from harassment and assault because the latter can result from a single incident or a small number of incidents, whereas bullying tends to be an accumulation of many small incidents over a long period of time.

The most despicable bullies on this earth are terrorists, murderers, rapists, paedophiles and pimps. These dregs of the earth all have one insatiable and obsessive need - to control others. They know of no other way to live life except to overpower others. However, they're cowards and have yellow streaks down their backbones. Anyone who feels confident about him- or herself does not need to use power to influence or control others.

This control is gained through terror, intimidation, harassment or just plain aggressiveness. The extrovert bullies tend to be shouters and screamers - are highly visible and bully from the top. A discussion becomes a debate and often ends up in a shouting match. They manipulate others into believing that they caused the bullying behaviour. Introverted bullies (the most dangerous types) tend to sit in the background and recruit others to do the bullying for them.

Bullies are cunning, conniving, scheming, calculating, sadistic, violent, cruel, nasty, ruthless, treacherous, pre-meditated, exploitive, parasitic, obnoxious, opportunist, ominous, menacing, sinister, ferocious, forceful, annoying, and aggressive. They are experts in the use of sarcasm but lack communication, interpersonal and social skills. Some rely excessively or exclusively on memos, emails or third parties and other strategies for avoiding face-to-face contact.

Rational human beings strive to coexist with others. Bullies don't understand this concept. Their need to control can reach obsessive heights and they can even have panic attacks if they feel they're not in control of every situation. These are sick people.

Bullies like pimps, relish having control over other human beings. However, they are insecure cowards whose only source of confidence is to be in control of situations and of others. This control is gained through terror, intimidation, harassment or just plain aggressiveness.

Bullies lack emotional intelligence. Emotional intelligence helps people understand and control their own emotions. It also helps them recognise and respond correctly to others' emotions. Those with emotional intelligence recognise emotions in others and know how to control their reactions to those emotions. They also know their own emotions and how to control them when they are getting upset or angry. Bullies are either born without emotional intelligence, or they suppress it by copying their defective role models. Often extensive counselling is the only way to change their destructive behaviour.

Abuse is defined in the dictionary as *'an evil or corrupt practice; deceit, betrayal, molestation, violation'* and comes in many forms. The common denominator of all abuse is the collection of behaviours related to bullying.

- Abusers *choose* to abuse,
- Molesters *choose* to molest,
- Rapists *choose* to rape,
- Harassers *choose* to harass,
- Paedophiles *choose* to abuse children, and
- Bullies *choose* to bully.

Symptoms of bullying

- Being belittled, demeaned or patronized especially in front of others. This chips away at the person's status, self-confidence, worth and potential;
- Being disgraced, shouted at and threatened, often in front of others;
- Making snide comments to see if the person will fight back;
- Finding fault and criticising everything the victim says and does or twisting, distorting and misrepresenting the victim. The criticism is of a trivial nature and often contains a grain of truth. This can dupe the victim into believing the criticism is valid.

- An unvarying refusal to recognise the victim's contributions;
- Treating them differently by showing favouritism to others and bias towards the victim.

Forms of bullying

- Terrorism and murder;
- Child abuse; child sexual abuse and child neglect;
- Pimping (selling of prostitution);
- Wife battering (domestic violence);
- School bullies;
- Armed forces bullying;
- Elderly abuse;
- Sports sexual abuse;
- Prison bullying;
- Road and queue rage;
- Stalking;
- Email abuse (on-line dating abuses);
- Neighbour abuse;
- Phone abuse;
- Cyber bullying;
- Workplace bullying;
- Sexual harassment: at work, at home, at school, in public (such as restaurants;
- Discrimination: age, sex, disabled, culture or nationality, religion;
- Mobbing (group bullying)

Where are people bullied?

- At home; (by parents, siblings or partners through bullying, assault, domestic violence, wife/child abuse, verbal abuse, neglect, emotional abuse);
- At school; (by other students, teachers or school staff);
- Under the care of others; (at child- or aged-care facilities – retirement villages – in hospitals, care homes, group homes, convalescent or rehabilitation facilities); At work; (by managers, clients, co-workers and subordinates through bullying / harassment, mobbing, falsifying time sheets, pilfering, embezzlement, fraud, malpractice, conspiracy, breaches of health and safety regulations, sexual harassment and/or discrimination);
- In prison; (by guards or other prisoners - by bullying, harassment, discrimination, assault);

- In the armed forces; (bullying, harassment, discrimination, assault);
- By those in authority; (harassment, abuse of power);
- By neighbours, landlords and even friends; (bullying, stalking, harassment);
- By strangers in restaurants and in line-ups; (that can involve harassment, stalking, assault, sexual assault, rape, grievous bodily harm, and even murder).
- On the road; (road rage).

Why do bullies bully?

Some bully because their role models (often their parents or older siblings) bully. It's natural for children to mimic the behaviour of these role models. Others seem to be born with a lack of empathy towards others or a feeling that they are superior to others. It's almost impossible for these individuals to understand what their bullying behaviour does to their victims. Only professional counselling (lasting sometimes for years) can reverse these flawed individuals.

Who are the targets of bullying?

It is often assumed that victims of bullying are weak and inadequate. Targets of bullying are assumed to be loners, but most are independent, self-reliant and have no need for gangs or cliques. They have neither a need to impress nor are they interested in office politics. Bullies select individuals who prefer to use dialogue to resolve conflict and who will go to great lengths to avoid conflict. They constantly try to use negotiation rather than resorting to grievance and legal action. Targets are chosen because they are competent and popular. Bullies are jealous of the easy and stable relationships targets have with others.

Many targets are so traumatised by the bullying that they need professional help or take stress leave until the incidence of bullying is investigated. Bullies love this because they can claim that their target is *'mentally ill'* or *'mentally unstable'* or has a *'mental health problem'*. It's much more likely that this allegation is a projection of the bully's own mental health problems which have not been treated.

Kinds of abuse

Bullying occurs in virtually all situations of life in which people interact with others. Thus, we have bullying at home, at school, by caregivers in various situations, at work, in prison, in the armed forces, as neighbours interact and in public places through stalking, assault and road rage.

In terms of abuse and criminal acts in general, there are glaring differences between the genders. Young men are more likely to commit murder, arson, assault, fraud and sexual and drug-related offenses. For such acts, male offenders typically outnumber female offenders 4 to 1. As many of the factors causing bullying and abuse also lead to these behaviours, we need to give proper guidance to our boys and young men.

Although this book is about school bullying, it is important to know the different kinds of abuse, because bullies are often abusive in many areas of their lives. There are many kinds of abuse:

Violence: this includes wife and child battering, violent crime such as murder and road rage. Intimidation and threats on the telephone or from neighbours are also a form of violence.

Bullying: This form of abuse occurs in schools, in prison, in the military and at the workplace. Elderly people and children may also be bullied because of their age.

Sexual abuse: Sexual harassment occurs at work, home, school, and in places such as restaurants. This form of abuse also includes child sexual harassment, rape in all its forms and online dating abuse.

Discrimination: This is done on grounds of age, sex, disability, culture, nationality and religion.

Other forms of abuse: These include child neglect, stalking, pornography, road rage, queue rage and arson.

Kinds of bullies

- Adult bullies in the workplace;
- Abusive and violent partners;
- Abusive and violent parents;
- Abusive and violent children (abuse their parents and others);
- Abusers of those in care;
- Bullying neighbours, landlords, authorities;
- Con artists and swindlers;
- Cult leaders;
- Child bullies who can grow up to be adult bullies;
- Racial and sexual harassers;
- Sexual abusers and paedophiles;

- Rapists (also date rape) and those who commit acts of sexual violence;
- Advocates of hard pornography;
- Stalkers;
- Arsonists;
- Violent offenders including organised serial killers.

They are also found in a variety of situations:

Physical Bullies:

They act out their anger in physical ways. They resort to hitting or kicking their victims or damaging the victim's property. Of all the types of bullies, this one is easiest to identify because his or her behaviour is so obvious. This is the type of bully our imagination conjures up when we picture a bully. As they get older, physical bullies can become more aggressive in their attacks. As adults this aggressive attitude is so deeply ingrained in the bully's personality that serious long-term counselling is required to change the behaviour.

Verbal Bullies:

It is quite difficult for a victim to ignore this type of bully. They use words to hurt and humiliate, resorting to name-calling, insulting, teasing and making racist, chauvinistic or paternalistic comments. While this type of bullying does not result in physical scars, its effects can be devastating. It is often the easiest form of attack for a bully. It is quick and painless for the bully, but often remarkably harmful for the victim.

Pornography:

Pornography has been a traditional outlet for sexual frustration, and probably always will be. Its acceptability is determined by current social values. Most people do not object to *'soft'* pornography and may even secretly indulge occasionally to see what they are missing. The harder the pornographic content, the more abusive it tends to be. The individual's need, and hence dependency on pornography is directly proportional to that individual's feelings of sexual inadequacy.

Female Bullies:

Society assumes that in a violent situation, there is a male aggressor and a female victim, but females can be as vicious as males. Female bullies are spiteful, devious, manipulative and vengeful. These individuals use gossip and backstabbing to undermine, discredit or devaluate other's contributions. They have poorly-defined moral and ethical boundaries and put others down to make themselves feel important. They are experts in the use of sarcasm but lack communication, interpersonal and social skills.

Group Bullies:

These are predominantly female bullies who exclude their victims from feeling part of a group. They exploit the feeling of insecurity in their victims, by ambushing their victims and convincing peers to exclude or reject the victim. They often use the same tricks that the verbal bullies use with their victims to isolate them. Spreading nasty rumours about the victim is part of the pattern. It can be an extremely harmful form of bullying especially in children when they are making their first social connections, because it excludes the victim from his or her peer group.

Bullies who were victims:

Some bullies have been bullied or abused themselves. There is evidence that many murderers, especially those involving serial killings, have received brain damage from parental beatings. Those beatings can leave them with the inability to control their violent tendencies.

The first-time bullies get a taste of their own medicine, they run whining to authorities for protection. They bully to feel competent, to get some relief from their own feelings of powerlessness. They are stuck between the state of a victim and a bully and are usually the most difficult to identify because they, at first glance, appear to be targets of other bullies and fiercely attack their bullies. They are usually impulsive and react quickly to intentional or unintentional physical encounters, claiming self-defence for their actions. Rather than lashing out at his or her bully, this victim needs to learn how to avoid other bullies.

Many abusers, molesters, harassers and bullies who end up in court because of their actions insist they were victims too.

These bullies seem to rely on their past problems as a victim to gain supporters. Such *'do-gooders'* will take advantage of any form of support they can get to evade taking responsibility for their actions. When asked to account for the way they choose to behave, bullies use a variety of strategies to evade accountability such as denial, counter-attack and feigned victimhood.

They are experts at buck-passing. They have not learned how to take responsibility for their actions, lack self-discipline, and will often blame someone else for why they reacted as they did.

Road Rage:

Bullies are also prone to road rage. Road rage occurs when one driver expresses his or her anger towards another driver for something s/he did on the road. People are encouraged to engage in road rage by the fact that they will not see each other again. They also feel that the other motorist is just some idiot who has endangered their lives. Road rage can be expressed through screaming, beeping the horn, flashing headlights, slamming on the brakes to teach a tailgater a lesson, cutting a person off to retaliate, throwing things, hostile stares, sticking out the middle finger, and profanities. Others even get out of their cars and start fighting.

Most people who demonstrate road rage are aggressive drivers, but do not consider their actions a problem to others. They think of the other drivers as being stupid, rude, and discourteous. The stresses of modern urban life are no reason to take it out on other drivers.

Stalkers:

Stalkers include intimate partner stalkers, delusional stalkers and vengeful stalkers. Studies show that the overwhelming number of stalkers is men and the overwhelming number of their victims is women.

Intimate partner stalkers refuse to believe that the relationship has ended. Most of these stalkers are not lonely people who are still hopelessly in love. On the contrary, they are emotionally abusive and controlling both during and after the relationship has ended. The only thing to say to the stalker is *'No'* once only, and then never say anything to him again. If the stalker cannot have his victim's love, he will settle for her hatred or her fear. The worst thing in the world for stalkers is to be ignored.

Delusional stalkers frequently have had little, if any, contact with their victims. They may have major illnesses like schizophrenia, manic-depression or erotomania. In erotomania, the stalker's delusional belief is that the victim loves him, and he believes that he is having a relationship even though they might never have met. Another more tenacious type might believe that he is destined to be with someone, and that if he only pursues her hard enough and long enough, she will come to love him. Most are unmarried and socially immature.

The vengeful stalker is driven by vengeance, rather than love. They become angry with their victims over some slight, either real or imagined. This could be anger at a politician because of some piece of legislation they introduced, or it could be disgruntled ex-employees.

Queue Rage

Public servants are being bashed, stalked and threatened with weapons in unprecedented abuse from customers forced to wait in long queues and being forced to fill in official forms. In one case they found the name of the person on the other side of the counter, found out where she lived and followed her. This employee's health has been destroyed and she will never be able to work again. Others have been threatened with syringes. Government employees at all levels are vulnerable to the danger. This could be classed as workplace abuse and their employers need to know this. By not having enough employees available to *'service'* their clients, they are setting their staff up for abuse by the clients.

The alarming increase in queue rage has prompted special training programs for frightened counter staff. This behaviour includes people jumping the counter, threatening, jumping the queue, and performing in the waiting area for the benefit of others. And the public servants are wilting. Society in general and clients being served by government staff are more aware of their rights now than ever before. This has made them become more assertive and they can become very angry when trying to get what they want.

Employees are being trained to recognise the danger signals. They see clients fuming and know something is happening. This is where an alert supervisor can anticipate trouble. Employees are given alarm bells and a system of security that they can use if the situation escalates into abusive behaviour.

Cyber Bullying

Cyber bullying occurs when an adult or child is tormented, threatened, harassed, humiliated, embarrassed or otherwise targeted by another adult or child, using the Internet, interactive and digital technologies or mobile phones.

Cyber bullying is usually not a one-time communication, unless it involves a death threat or a credible threat of serious bodily harm. In extreme cases people have killed each other or committed suicide after being involved in a cyber bullying incident.

Penalties for Cyber Bullying

Most of the time the cyber bullying does not go so far that the law intervenes, although victims often might attempt to lodge criminal charges. Cyber bullying however, may result in a misdemeanour cyber harassment charge, or if the bullying child is young enough may result in the charge of juvenile delinquency. It must have a minor on both sides, or at least have been instigated by a minor against another minor.

It typically can result in the person losing their ISP or IM accounts because they violated their terms of service rules. In some cases, if hacking or password and identity theft is involved, they can be charged with serious criminal charges by state and federal law enforcement agencies.

Cyber Bullying is NOT...

Once adults cyber bully children, it is called **cyber harassment or cyber stalking.**

Adult cyber-harassment or cyber stalking is not cyber bullying.

It isn't when adults are trying to lure children into offline meetings. That is called **sexual exploitation** or luring by a sexual predator. The methods used are limited only by the bully's imagination and access to technology. And the cyber bully one moment may become the victim the next. They often change roles, going from victim to bully and back again.

Preventing Cyber Bullying

Educating the kids about the consequences (losing their ISP or IM accounts) helps. Teaching them to respect others and to take a stand against bullying of all kinds helps too. Because their motives differ, the solutions and responses to each type of cyber bullying incident must differ too. Schools can work with parents to stop and remedy cyber bullying. They can also educate the students on cyber-ethics and the law. If schools are creative, they can sometimes avoid the claim that their actions exceeded their legal authority for off-campus cyber-bullying actions.

Because their motives differ, the solutions and responses to each type of cyber bullying incident must differ too. Schools can work with parents to stop and remedy cyber bullying. They can also educate the students on cyber-ethics and the law. If schools are creative, they can sometimes avoid the claim that their actions exceeded their legal authority for off-campus cyber-bullying actions.

Parents also need to understand that a child is just as likely to be a cyber bully as a victim of cyber bullying and often go back and forth between the two roles during one incident. They may not even realize that they are a cyber bully.

Update:

In 2018 the Queensland Department of Education is in the process of implementing a British software product eSafe Global, which is used to track the activities of known sex offenders. It will be trialled in four independent schools. This product captures everything students do on school computers or laptops: even the images they view offline or the words they type into draft documents. This allows principals and teachers to be alerted if serious risks are found, including cases of cyber bullying, pornography, threats of self-harm, terrorist or drug associations. The software is already being used by 9000 students in Western Australia and almost 800,000 students in the United Kingdom.

How you can stop Cyber Bullying once it starts

There are two things parents must consider before anything else. Is your child at risk of physical harm or assault? And how are they handling the attacks emotionally?

If there is any indication that personal contact information has been posted online, or any threats are made to your child, you must run, do not walk, to your local law enforcement agency. Take a print-out of all instances of cyber bullying to show them but note that a print-out is not sufficient to prove a case of cyber-harassment or cyber bullying. You'll need electronic evidence and live data for that. It is crucial that all electronic evidence be preserved to allow the person to be traced and to take whatever action needs to be taken. The electronic evidence is at risk for being deleted by the Internet service providers unless you notify them immediately that you need those records preserved!

Parents need to be the ones students trust when things go wrong online and offline. Yet students often don't go to their parents. Why? It's because their parents tend to over-react. Most children will avoid telling their parents about a cyber bullying incident fearing they will only make things worse.

Unfortunately, they also sometimes under-react. They need to be supportive of their children and realize that these attacks can follow them into their otherwise safe home and wherever they go online. The risk of emotional pain is very real, and very serious, so parents should not ignore their plight.

Sports Bullying

A recent report released in Italy on violence in sport by UNICEF, said nearly one in ten Australians had suffered sexual abuse in a sporting context. Sexual violence against children in sport in Australia could be as high as 8 per cent compared to Canada, where 2.6 per cent of children reported experiencing unwanted sexual touching.

Trisha Layhee, one of the report's authors said the rates of sexual violence may be much higher and work was needed to assess the issue. Dr. Layhee, who now heads the Hong Kong Sports Institute, said Australia was unique in the world for having a coaching culture that encouraged extreme psychological abuse.

"What we found was the complete normalization of psychologically abusive behaviour by coaches, particularly at the elite level. I mean coaches screaming at kids," she said.

Her survey of 370 elite and club athletes in Australia found 31 per cent of female and 21 per cent of male athletes reported sexual abuse under the age of 18. Of these, 41 per cent of females and 29 per cent of males said the abuse occurred in a sporting context.

Chapter 2

HEALTH DISORDERS ASSOCIATED WITH SCHOOL BULLYING

Diagnosis of abusers is challenging. How do you deal with a person who is a compulsive liar with a Jekyll and Hyde nature, is charming and glib, excels at deception and evasion of accountability?

Many abusers fit the criteria for ***Antisocial Personality Disorder (APD).*** Although most people think those with APD are associated with low socio-economic status and urban settings and tend to be of lower intelligence - this is not the case. They come from all environments.

These individuals have a complete disregard for and violate the rights of others and indicate at least three of the following symptoms:

- Fail to conform to social norms with respect to lawful behaviours by performing acts that are grounds for arrest;
- Deceitful by repeated lying, use of aliases, and conning others for personal profit or pleasure;
- Impulsiveness - fail to see the consequences of their actions;
- Irritability and aggressiveness, indicated by repeated physical fights, assaults or verbal battles;
- Reckless disregard for the safety of self or others;
- Consistently irresponsible - repeated failure to sustain consistent work behaviour;
- Fail to honour their financial obligations;
- Lack remorse by being indifferent to, or rationalizing having hurt, mistreated, or stolen from others;
- Belong to gangs and cliques that do not only appear in school-aged children, but at the highest executive level in business.

Many serial bullies would also meet many, if not all, of the clinical criteria for a ***Psychopath.*** Psychopaths lack remorse, guilt and conscience. Although many psychopaths meet the diagnostic criteria for antisocial personality disorder; not all do. Similarly, not all people with antisocial personality disorder meet the criteria for a psychopath. Not all psychopaths end up in prison. Industrial Psychopaths can thrive in business and many are found in management or executive positions.

The serial bully displays behaviour congruent with many of the diagnostic criteria for **Narcissistic Personality Disorder.** This is shown by a pervasive pattern of grandiosity and self-importance, the need for admiration and for the lack of empathy. People with this disorder overestimate their abilities and inflate their accomplishments, often appearing boastful and pretentious, have fantasies of unlimited success and/or power, while correspondingly underestimate and devalue the achievements and accomplishments of others.

They're contemptuous, envious and impatient with others and take advantage of others to achieve their own ends. They need power, prestige, drama and enjoy manipulating others. These qualities draw them top leadership positions, but at extreme levels of narcissism - the results can be disastrous.

Narcissists can become intolerant of criticism, unwilling to compromise, and frequently surround themselves with sycophants (flatterers). While narcissists often appear to be ideal choices for leadership positions, they may fall victim to the distortions of their narcissistic tendencies that are reinforced by their position.

Some will fraudulently claim to have qualifications, experience, affiliations or associations that they don't have or are not entitled to. They have low self-esteem and need constant attention and admiration. They fish for compliments, expect superior service and for others to defer to them. They lack sensitivity and empathy especially when others don't react in the expected manner. They expect to receive before and above the needs of others, and overwork those around them. They may form romantic or sexual relationships for advancing their purpose or career, abuse special privileges, and squander resources.

A **Sociopath** is an individual with many characteristics of APD and expresses his/her violence psychologically through constant criticism, sidelining, exclusion, undermining, etc. Sociopaths are usually highly intelligent, have higher socio-economic status, and often come from middle-class families.

The term *'psychosis'* is applied to mental illness, and the term *'neuroses'* to psychiatric injury. The main difference is that a psychotic person is unaware they have a mental problem whereas the neurotic person is aware - often acutely. The serial bully's lack of insight into his/her behaviour and its effect on others has the hallmarks of a psychosis, although this obliviousness would appear to be a choice, rather than a condition. They show these behaviours:

- Are very controlling of others. If someone resists, they are vicious in their attack to regain that control.
- They don't listen to others, lack conscience, show no remorse, are drawn to power, are emotionally cold and flat, dysfunctional, disruptive, divisive, rigid and inflexible, selfish, insincere, insecure, immature, and lack interpersonal skills.
- They are vicious, criticizing and vindictive in private - but charming in front of witnesses. (Others often don't see this side of their nature).
- Are very convincing or compulsive liars and when called upon, can fabricate authentic-sounding reasons for their behaviour.
- Are charming and convincing, which they use to make up for their lack of empathy.
- Hiding under their charming exterior is often sexual harassment, discrimination and racial prejudice.
- On the surface they seem very self-assured, but inside are very insecure people.
- They excel at deception - have vivid imaginations - are often very creative.
- They encourage feelings of shame, embarrassment, guilt and fear, for that is how all abusers - including child sex abusers – control and silence their victims.
- Show inappropriate attitudes to sexual matters or behaviour.
- Refuse to acknowledge, value or praise others.
- When others describe their uncaring nature, they respond with impatience, irritability and aggression.
- Often have an overwhelming, unhealthy and narcissistic need to portray themselves as a wonderful, kind, caring and compassionate person, in contrast to their behaviour and treatment of others.
- Are oblivious to the discrepancy between how they like to be seen (and believe they are seen) and how they are actually seen.
- Are unaware of leadership qualities (maturity, decisiveness, assertiveness, trust and integrity) and bullying (immaturity, impulsiveness, aggression, distrust and deceitfulness).
- When called to account for their actions, they aggressively deny everything, and then counter-attack with distorted or fabricated

criticism and allegations. If this is insufficient, they quickly feign being the victim, often bursting into tears (the purpose is to avoid answering the question and thus evade accountability by manipulating others using guilt).

Some serial bullies show signs of passive/aggressive behaviour. These people can be very dangerous. They have a pathological reaction to authority and those they perceive are in positions of authority. They channel their aggression into passive behaviour by slowing down efforts of others and stonewall progress. They're very hard to detect, and others often feel frustrated when dealing with them but don't always understand why.

As most of us grow up, we're faced with restrictions that are normal and necessary. People with this tendency have often been controlled excessively, so the person learns to control others without confrontation. They love the thrill of insubordination, and it sometimes doesn't matter if they win, if it appears their opponents loose. They love to play win-lose games and put something over on others.

They use excuses such as: *"It's not my fault this didn't work, it's yours."* They show frequent signs of helplessness - the simplest thing seems beyond their comprehension. They provoke a feeling of defensiveness when others are dealing with them. Most tasks are performed late or not at all. When prodded they become argumentative. They're backstabbers, gossipers and are often so good at it that others believe their falsehoods.

Most people display the above signs at one time or another. However, if this develops into being their normal behaviour, these people are likely passive-aggressive, and others will have to remain on guard when dealing with them. Make sure they understand the consequences of their actions, *"If this happens again, I'll..."* Confront them using facts when you *'catch them in the act.'*

Some serious passive-aggressives have criminal tendencies. Although they insist that others adhere to the rules of society, they have an unwillingness to conform, believing these do not apply to them. These people get a thrill out of speeding, of drinking and driving - and getting away with it. In some, this tendency keeps accelerating because they require higher and higher levels of danger, thrills and excitement to keep them appeased.

The Gender Differences

The statistics for criminal actions are staggering and identify that we're not giving the proper guidance to our boys and young men:

- Young men have a 300 per cent higher death rate from motor vehicle accidents than young women;
- Jail inmates - 95 per cent male - 5 per cent female;
- Homicide - 85 per cent male - 15 per cent female;
- Arson - 86 per cent male - 14 per cent female;
- Assault - 82 per cent male - 18 per cent female;
- Sexual offences - 98 per cent male - 2 per cent female;
- Manslaughter by driving - 80 per cent male – 20 per cent female;
- Malicious damage to property - 87 per cent male – 13 per cent female;
- Blackmail - 92 per cent male - 8 per cent female;
- Drug offences - 82 per cent male - 18 per cent female;
- Fraud - 63 per cent male - 37 per cent female;
- Shoplifting - 60 per cent male - 40 per cent female.

What are the results to the victim/target of bullying?

- The victims' constant high stress level interferes with their immune system causing frequent illnesses such as the flu, ulcers, irritable bowel problems, skin problems such as eczema, psoriasis, athlete's foot, shingles, colds, coughs, ear, nose and throat infections.
- Their body's batteries never have an opportunity to recharge.
- They suffer from aches and pains in the joints and muscles or have back pain with no obvious cause that won't go away or respond to treatment.
- They're disempowered such that they become dependent on the bully to allow them to get through each day without their life being made hell.
- Initially they're reluctant to act against their bullies and report them knowing that they could accelerate the abuse. Later this gives way to a strong urge to act against the bullies so that others don't have to suffer a similar fate.

The targets have:

- An overwhelming desire for acknowledgement, understanding, recognition and validation of their experience and strong motivation for justice to be done;
- An unwillingness to talk or interact with the bully;
- An unusually strong sense of vulnerability, victimisation or persecution;
- An unusually strong desire to educate the public and help the public introduce domestic violence and child abuse prevention laws;
- An overwhelming sense of betrayal and an inability or unwillingness to trust anyone;
- Headaches and migraines;
- Shattered self-confidence and low self-esteem;
- Become seriously depressed, especially upon waking;
- Become tired, exhausted and lethargic;
- Found their levels of guilt are abnormally high which may preclude them from starting new relationships;
- Found themselves constantly fatigued (like Chronic Fatigue Syndrome), or sweat, tremble, shake, or have heart palpitations;
- Suffered from panic attacks triggered by any reminder of the experience;
- Physical numbness (toes, fingertips, lips) and emotional numbness (especially the inability to feel joy);
- Impaired memory that's due to suppressing horrific memories;
- Found they're constantly on edge mentally – have a short fuse and are irritated, especially by small insignificant events;
- Often been highly upset by the amount of anger they feel towards their abuser and are horrified by the mental pictures of creative, cruel, torturous ways they could pay back their abuser;
- Constantly been on alert because their fight or flight mechanism has become permanently activated;
- Become hypersensitive and inappropriately perceive almost any remark as critical;
- Found that work becomes difficult, often impossible to undertake;
- Become obsessed with the abusive experience that takes over their lives, eclipsing and excluding almost every other interest;
- Believed that their abusive problems are hopeless and that their efforts to stop it will be futile;

- Been sleepless, have nightmares, constantly relive events, wake early or wake up more tired than when they went to bed;
- Poor concentration and become forgetful especially with trivial day-to-day things;
- Experienced regular intrusive, violent visualisations and flashbacks and can't get the abuse out of their minds;
- Become emotional - bursting into tears regularly over trivial matters;
- Become uncharacteristically irritable, have angry outbursts, are hypersensitive and feel fragile;
- Feelings of withdrawal and isolation, want to be on their own and seek solitude;
- Suffered from post-traumatic stress disorder (PTSD).

Post-traumatic stress following victimisation is largely due to the shattering of basic assumptions victims hold about themselves and the world. Specifically, that:

- The world is kind, caring, compassionate, generous, giving;
- The world is meaningful;
- I am worthy.

For the targets that become victims of abuse, their world and self-view is shattered, and they may find it impossible to function normally or effectively. Research would indicate that often those who suffer most from unacceptable abusive behaviour are those with the most to give - those with high expectations of themselves and those who are prepared to go the extra mile because they believe that what they do is meaningful and important.

What is Post Traumatic Stress Disorder (PTSD)?

David Kinchin estimates in his book *Post Traumatic Stress Disorder: the Invisible injury* www.bullyonline.org/stress/davidk.htm that at any time, around one per cent of the population are experiencing PTSD. Within some groups of society, the incidence of PTSD must be expected to be much higher than one per cent.

Post-Traumatic Stress Disorder PTSD is a natural emotional reaction to a deeply shocking and disturbing experience. There is growing recognition that PTSD can result from many types of shocking experiences including an accumulation of small, individually non-life-threatening events. These situations are called Complex PTSD. The individual experiencing trauma feels s/he is unable to escape the situation. Traumatic situations of domestic, school and workplace abuse can be extremely difficult to get out of.

Sometimes those who are abused thinks they are going mad. They are not; PTSD is an injury, not an illness. The silent suffering could be considerable, but those who suffer - mostly unnecessarily - are prevented from realising their potential and contributing fully to society and to industry. Many sufferers of Complex PTSD are hard workers who are reluctant to claim health benefits.

Depression

Stress, or more appropriately *'distress'* occurs when an individual believes that the demands or perceived demands of a situation outweigh his/her ability or perceived ability to cope with the situation. The coping mechanisms under challenge include those the person needs to resolve the problem, be it emotional, familial, work-related or otherwise. From a psychological viewpoint, depression occurs when the individual feels his/her world is consistently unpleasant, punishing or deprives them of the opportunity for a positive and satisfying life. Their negative experiences may be compounded by feelings of being unable to change their situation - a process of learned helplessness.

Individuals with depression expect and predict that their unpleasant and distressing experiences will continue. Guilt-ridden perceptions of being responsible for their own distress, either through the things they have done or not done, or negative thoughts about their inability to cope, add to the depressed feelings. The combination of a negative view of their lives, the expectation that it will continue, the self-criticism or self-blame for the situation, coupled with the inability to cope, are the characteristic psychological processes of depression.

Stress Breakdown

Stress breakdown differs from a nervous breakdown or mental breakdown that are the consequence of mental illness. Stress breakdown is a psychiatric injury, which is a normal reaction to an abnormal situation. The two types of breakdown are distinct and should not be confused. A stress breakdown is a natural and normal conclusion to a period of prolonged negative stress; the body is saying:

"I'm not designed to operate under these conditions of prolonged negative stress so I'm going to do something dramatic to ensure that you reduce or eliminate the stress. Otherwise, my body may suffer irreparable damage and I must take action now."

Dr. John T. O'Brien, consultant in old-age psychiatry at Newcastle General Hospital published a paper subtitled: *'Prolonged stress may cause permanent brain damage'.*

A stress breakdown is often predictable, sometimes days or weeks in advance. The person's fear, fragility, obsessiveness, hyper-vigilance and hypersensitivity combine to evolve into paranoia. If this happens, a stress breakdown is only days or even hours away and the person needs urgent medical help. The risk of suicide at this point is heightened. Research says that young men are committing suicide at five times the rate as females.

Self-Harm

Self-harm is linked to abuse, unwanted pregnancy and parental divorce. One in 17 children is believed to hurt or self-harm itself. Behind these children is often a family in distress. Self-harm is the intentional cause to harm one's own body. These include: deliberate self-harm, self-injury, self-mutilation, self-abuse, self-wounding, self-inflicted violence, para-suicide, non-fatal act, and wrist cutting. All these definitions of self-harm cover the same actions:

- Cutting;
- Burning skin by physical means using heat;
- Burning skin by chemical means using caustic liquids;
- Punching hard enough to cause bruises;
- Head banging;
- Hair pulling from head, eyelashes, eyebrows and armpits;
- Poisoning by ingesting small amounts of toxic substances to cause discomfort or damage;
- Insertion of foreign objects;
- Excessive nail biting to the point of bleeding and ripping cuticles;
- Excessive scratching by removing top layer of skin to cause a sore;
- Bone breaking;
- Gnawing at flesh;
- Wound interference to prevent wounds from healing thus prolonging the effect;
- Tying ligatures around the neck, arms or legs to restrict the flow of blood;
- Medication abuse without intention to die;
- Alcohol abuse;

- Illegal drug use;
- Smoking.

Cutting and burning are among the most common forms of self-harm. Those who are smoking and drinking, are not consciously harming themselves; they are taking part in a socially accepted lifestyle. It is only once these actions become excessive that problems can occur.

There is also a strong correlation between eating disorders and self-harm. This is because starvation, binge-eating and self-induced vomiting, overuse of laxatives and diuretics, are forms of self-harm, as are starvation, binge-eating and vomiting.

Chapter 3

BULLYING AT SCHOOL

'Kids will be kids' or *'boys will be boys'* was often the response by adults when a child complained about bullying. But we now know that bullying is assault, and victims are protected by law when that happens. Bullies learn young that words can be used to hurt - so they experiment. They want to experience the feeling of power that comes with being able to manipulate some-one. For some kids, it is something they try once. In others it becomes a way of life and every situation becomes a power struggle - with their parents, their teachers, their siblings and their playmates.

The bully does not have to be the nicest, best-looking or the funniest kid. S/he just needs to know how to form a group and then take charge. They make the rules and decide whether they will play with a new kid or make his/her life miserable via bullying.

One daughter was caught shoplifting. The family was horrified but were even more upset months later when the full story was revealed. The girl was stealing to avoid being attacked by a bully. She was ordered to steal, told what to steal, and if she didn't bring the goods to school - she was in for it. The fact that the bully had so much control over the girl that she would take the chance of being arrested to avoid a bully, should tell us the power these bullies have over others.

Even though Australia was voted the number one destination in the world for young people to come for work or study and they were told Australia was a safe, bright country, they have been beaten so badly that they had to go home. A recent survey of visiting students found that more and more are experiencing violence, racism and discrimination. Students locked themselves in their dorms fearing violence on the streets. The most troubling location was metropolitan Sydney.

Australian university students have recently been called anti-Asian and anti-USA because of the violence they have shown towards foreign students. With over 225,000 international students in Australian universities, this could be devastating. Students have gone home to Korea and Japan fearing their lives because of mindless violence outside Curtin University in Perth.

American students have left Queensland universities because of the anger against US President George W. Bush and the war in Iraq. Some suffered culture shock (because of the belief that everyone loved Americans) and students were advised not to carry any items that would identify their nationality. Ian Wanner 19 from Oregon attended Griffith University (that has a zero-tolerance policy to harassment) and had abusive students repeatedly calling him *'sepo'* - short for septic tank. A female student said she was going home to America in shock over her treatment. Queensland university students are showing open hostility, and, in some cases, US students and academics are being persecuted for merely having an American accent.

Differences between child and adult bullying

There are two main differences:

An adult is selected for bullying because they are good at their job and popular with people (the bully is a weak, inadequate individual who is driven by jealousy and envy). If there is a child in the class who is socially less popular than the rest, then this child is likely to be targeted by the bully. If no such obvious child exists, then the bully will pick on any child they think is unable or unwilling to fight. A key factor in the bully's choice is any child who is unwilling to resort to violence to resolve conflict - in other words, a child who has integrity and good moral codes. Given that bullies are driven by jealousy and envy, any child who is bright and popular is also likely to be targeted. Parents, teachers and carers must ensure that these children know how to deal with bullying.

Once bullying starts, many children will side with, or appear to side with, the bully because they know that otherwise they themselves will be bullied.

The bully is a deeply unpopular child with whom other children associate, not through friendship, but through fear.

Many studies that show bullies to be popular fail to make this distinction. Also, the education system is biased towards physical strength (i.e. undue emphasis on sport and rewards for sporting achievement) while artistic achievements are undervalued. Children (and adults) who are bullied tend to be imaginative, creative, caring and responsible. Children (and adults) who bully are unimaginative, uncaring, aggressive, emotionally immature, inadequate (especially in social skills) and irresponsible.

There is a lot anecdotal evidence to suggest that the child who learns to bully at school, *and who gets away with it,* then goes on to be the serial bully in the workplace.

The evidence suggests that the child who is bullied at school also goes on to be a likely target of bullying in the workplace.

This has nothing to do with being predisposed to being bullied - it has to do with the innate qualities of good people.

By the time a person enters adulthood at around the age of 18, their behaviour patterns are set and only time or a traumatic experience can alter these patterns. However, people who are likely to be bullied have a considerable learning capability and thus have a greater capacity to modify their behaviour as an adult. People who are bullies or prone to have limited learning capacity (especially in interpersonal and behavioural skills) will often exhibit bullying behaviours for the rest of their lives.

Emotionally, the bully remains a young child, and their attention-seeking behaviour is characteristic of a two-year-old throwing a temper tantrum to gain attention. Serial bullies have psychopathic or sociopathic tendencies that include a learning blindness and an apparent lack of insight into their behaviour and its effect on others. The second major difference between adult and child bullying is that the child bully can be helped to develop better ways of behaving providing that:

- Everyone knows and understands what bullying is and why bullies bully;
- Everyone knows and understands that bullying is unacceptable;
- Incidents of bullying are nipped in the bud;
- The bully is called to account in a firm, but kind and supportive manner *without* physical punishment (the child bully is usually deeply unhappy and has very low self-esteem);
- The bully is subsequently supervised and supported in learning more appropriate ways of interacting with other children;
- All children are taught how to be assertive;
- All children are taught how to spot bullying and intercede or report it;
- All children are empowered to help both target and bully;

This is where society needs to place its emphasis - on helping these children develop into better adults.

The child bully often (although not always) comes from a dysfunctional aggressive home environment where s/he is learning by example. Remember also that bullying (like abuse with which it is closely associated) is independent of class or financial status.

Dealing with School Bullying

Bullying is one of the most underrated and enduring problems in school today and only about one incident in twenty-five is reported. It can leave deep psychological scars and even drive children to suicide. We hear more about bullies these days because the incidents are bloodier and the consequences more terrifying. No more is it just a bloodied nose or black eye at recess, now we hear of guns, knives, murders and suicides. Something about the bullying we hear about these days feels different. It's not always the mean big kid beating up the scared little kid. It's often six or seven kids beating up one scared little kid. Or extorting lunch money, stealing jackets, or six or seven girls *'swarming'* and beating the girl who doesn't *'fit in.'*

Did you know that some well-known stars were bullied at school? **Whitney Houston** reports having bad memories of school because she was teased about her looks by some girls. **Michelle Pfeiffer** was also teased about her looks especially her lips and was nicknamed Michelle Mudturtle. She is reported as saying that at first, she ran home crying. She later fought back: *"I became a bully and a tomboy and used to beat up all the boys."* (Rynning, 3/4/93, New Idea, p.10), **Tom Cruise and Kevin Costner say they were bullied** because they had to change schools a lot. Tom Cruise was also given a hard time about having a learning problem. He was suspended from school for getting into fights. **Mel Gibson** moved to Australia from New York when he was 12. He was taunted for being chubby and because of his American accent. Mel Gibson is reported as saying that, *"At first, no one liked me; they made rude remarks about me, cut me to the bone ... My sense of humour kept the bullies away."* (Rynning, 3/4/93, New Idea, p.11)

Bullying occurs on average every seven minutes, and each bullying episode lasts about 37 seconds. Sixty per cent of children identified as bullies before they are eight years old, will have a criminal conviction by the age of twenty-four, so it's important that parents, teachers and the community do something to curb their bullying. If the bullies don't end up in jail, they'll end up involved in other violent behaviour like workplace bullying or spousal abuse.

According to a recent survey, bullying is not restricted to Western nations... some 94 per cent of Chinese students feel unsafe in school as the incidence of violence and bullying rise.

Joe, who lives in Cape Breton, sent his son to the Sydney Academy. He had picked that school because of its zero-tolerance bullying policy - but the system let him down. When his teen-aged son told him that he wanted to kill himself rather than put up with any more bullying at school, he and his wife were shocked and devastated. They had missed the early signs, a change in attitude and behaviour - because their son was covering up. After comforting his son and wife - the father called the police and laid charges against the bully. Shortly after Joe and his family moved away from Cape Breton to a new and safer school environment.

What constitutes school bullying?

Most children joke around with each other, call each other games or rough-house - and yet these incidents are not normally called bullying. The difference lies in the relationship of the bully and the victim and the intent of that interaction. It normally occurs between individuals who are *not* friends. There's a power difference between the bully and the victim. The bully is usually bigger, tougher, physically stronger, or can intimidate others.

Bullies and their victims come from all levels of socio-economic situations. Essentially, they're looking for power that they're not getting or feeling anywhere else. Bullying is gender-neutral and can range from gang attacks to playground bullying. Researchers still can't explain why young girls act out their aggression in different ways from boys, but their biology is believed to be the main factor. Girls use whispering campaigns and psycho-logical bullying that their teachers find hard to detect. With girls, it mainly comes in the form of gossiping, spreading lies, backbiting, ruining reputations, or social isolation that excludes one or more children from their group. Girls may be biologically hot-wired to engage in sophisticated, non-violent forms of aggression that can hurt just as much as a punch in the jaw from a boy. It's now believed that the non-physical conflict or indirect aggression could be as dangerous to children as physical bullying.

When caught, many girls use tactics such as apologising or crying - that gets them out of trouble but doesn't solve the underlying problem causing their bullying. Their targets feel that the bullying was directed towards excluding them from their peer group. Girls have different responses to authority than boys and in the way they deal with problems. They're more likely to skip school when problems arise. Many use truancies to deal with their bullies and often their teachers miss the real reason for their truancy. All truancy should be investigated to find the reasons behind the absence from school. Boys tend to defend themselves and answer back but can get themselves into worse trouble. Bullying amongst boys is usually physical and involves hitting and shoving.

For the child growing up in a dysfunctional or abusive home environment, bullying becomes a compulsive and obsessive behaviour. The bully must have a target, so s/he can displace his or her own aggression. The bullying child's parents may lack parental skills because they were brought up by parents who lacked appropriate behaviour skills, and their parents were brought up in that same climate. The cycle must be broken. This is where schools can play a major role - *but only if they enforce anti-bullying policies and support the bullied child.*

Children who pick on other children could come from dysfunctional homes or homes with a lack of adult supervision. They could be victims of violence themselves, learning that violence is an acceptable way to interact with others, or they could have missed a stage in their development and experienced a delay in their emotional development. Bullies may have parents who ignored them or parents who have mothers who abused alcohol or drugs while they were pregnant. Violent television programs also reinforce that it's okay to act aggressively.

Ultimately though, bullying is behaviour and behaviour is a choice. Therefore, bullying is a choice. It is the bully's choice to bully. A bad choice – but a choice! While a poor home environment, poor parenting, poor role models may influence the bully - they are not a cause. Many children have poor home environments but do not choose to bully; therefore, these factors cannot be used as a specific excuse for bullying.

The memory of individual school yard bullying remains clear and unblemished for many adults long after they leave school. Any child or adult can tell you about a time s/he was bullied, or s/he saw someone they knew being bullied. Bullies seek power. Bullying can be multiple episodes or consist of one single interaction. The intention of the bully is to put the victim in distress in some way.

Why are some children bullied?

When bullying is reported, or violent incidents or suicide hit the headlines, the reason the child was bullied is often highlighted as a principal cause of the bullying. In fact, the reason is spurious and specious (plausibly deceptive).

Reasons for being picked on include being fat, thin, tall, short, hair or skin colour, being quiet, wearing glasses, having big ears, small ears, sticky-out ears, crooked teeth, being from a different culture, having different likes or dislikes, the *'wrong clothes, unwillingness to use strength to defend him or herself, or any perceived or fabricated excuse'.* These excuses have one thing in common: ***they are all irrelevant!***

Each reason is a deceptive justification for the bully to indulge in a predictable pattern of violent (physical or psychological) behaviour against another child who is smaller, younger or less strong than the bully. The target is simply a useful object where the bully can displace his or her aggression. In other words, if a child is picked on because they are allegedly *'fat,'* then losing weight will make no difference; the bully simply invents another justification. If children are bullied for their dinner money, then introducing cashless swipe cards will make no difference; the bullies invent other reasons.

Do not be deceived into thinking that the reason for bullying has any validity; it does not. Ignore it. Helping your child to lose weight or have cosmetic surgery or wear the *'in'* fashions will make no difference. If you acknowledge the reason (i.e. telling overweight children to diet so they won't be bullied), you are unwittingly according the bully justification. Focus instead on why the bullying child needs to bully.

To tackle bullying you will have to liaise closely with the school and will probably have to talk to the bully's parents. Establish first whether this is an isolated incident (in which case nipping it in the bud is likely to have a high probability of success) or whether the child bully has a history of bullying behaviour. Remember that most children will try bullying at some time (including yours!); most will realise that it's not an appropriate way of behaving and grow out of it quickly, especially if you help your child see why it's inappropriate and encourage and support them in learning better ways of behaving.

However, for the child growing up in a dysfunctional or abusive home environment, bullying becomes a compulsive and obsessive behaviour; the bully needs to have a target onto whom s/he can displace his or her own aggression. The bullying child's parents may lack parental skills because they were brought up by parents who lacked appropriate behaviour skills, and their parents were brought up in that climate, etc. The cycle must be broken. This is where schools can play a major role. Helping parents adopt better parenting skills can also make a major difference if this is done tactfully.

Ultimately, bullying is behaviour and behaviour is a choice. Therefore, bullying is a choice. Whilst a poor home environment, poor parenting, poor role models etc may be influencing factors in bullying, they are not a cause. Many children have poor home environments etc but do not choose to bully; therefore, these factors cannot be used as a specious excuse for bullying. It is the bully's choice to bully, a bad choice, but a choice.

Why aren't all children bullied? Most victims of bullying are approached early in their schooling, or when they start a new school. Their first encounter with the bully usually determines whether the bully will approach them again. Children who are regularly victims of bullying tend to display *'vulnerable behaviours'* when they react to their bully. Those behaviours in turn inspire the bully to continue with his or her attacks. Children who are more prone to be picked on by a bully often possess the following characteristics:

- Low self-esteem;
- Insecure;
- Lack social skills;
- Cry or become upset easily; and
- Have not learned the skills to defend or stand up for themselves.

Schools are a prime location for bullying. Most of school bullying occurs in or close to school buildings. Many bullies try to pass off acts of aggression as roughhousing. Most victims don't report the bullying. Occasionally, a victim provokes the attack of their bully. These victims tease their bullies, making themselves a target by egging the bully on. These victims often don't know when to stop their provocation and usually aren't able to defend themselves when the balance of power shifts to the bully. Body language is everything when school bullies pick their prey.

Physical defects, like big ears, speech problems or a limp, don't normally play a role, but body language and level of self-esteem have every-thing to do with whether the child will or will not be bullied. Victims are encouraged to stand tall, say, *'No'* in a loud voice and make eye contact. If victims are taught how to react, they can curb the problem. A bully needs an audience, but if witnesses simply leave the area when a situation happens they report the bullying - the bullies lose their audience and must account for their behaviour.

Only twenty-five per cent of students report that teachers intervene in bullying situations, while seventy-one per cent of teachers believe they always intervene.

Research shows us that most students (60 per cent) are never directly involved in any kind of bullying, as victims or as bullies (Psychology

Today, September 1996). That said, most students have witnessed bullying incidents at the schoolyard. The unfortunate thing is they do nothing to stop the bullying.

Bullies are often socially accepted until their mid-teens. Despite their aggressive behaviour, they can even enjoy social popularity with their peers. But, by late adolescence, the bully's popularity begins to fade. Bullies lose their popularity as they get older and are eventually disliked by most students. The paths of the mid-teen bully and his or her former victim rarely cross. By that age, teens have clearly defined their social set. Tragically, the bully finds him or herself becoming more excluded by their peers and often seeks out alliances with gangs of other isolated individuals. These teen gangs often get into serious trouble with the law and others.

By senior high school, most regular bullying incidents are a thing of the past, but the memories of their abuse haunts victims and they continue to avoid their bully. Some carry their emotional scars for a lifetime.

Sixty percent of people who are identified as childhood bullies have at least one criminal conviction by the age of twenty-four. Those who carry their bullying behaviour with them into adulthood often develop a roster of problems: alcoholism, anti-social personality disorders and mental health disorders. If his or her behaviour is not treated, the bully can grow up to bully their spouses, children and co-workers. Bullying becomes a habit, an easy method for the bully to get what s/he wants.

The children who manage to ward off the bully tend to have better social and conflict management skills. So, this is where parents and teachers should place their emphasis in teaching children interpersonal skills. These children are better able to assert themselves without becoming aggressive or confrontational. Instead, they work out compromises and devise alternative solutions. These children appear to be more aware of people's feelings (empathetic skills) and are the children who can be most helpful in resolving disputes and assisting other children to get help.

Children who have been repeatedly victimised by a bully show certain behaviours and attitudes. Sometimes these behaviours are inconsistent with the child's typical behaviour. Many children are too embarrassed and humiliated to report victimisation and worry that speaking out will lead to more abuse.

Adolescent psychologist, **Michael Carr-Gregg** said South Australian research showed one in six young people was bullied weekly. He said bullying was one of the major contributors to psychological problems in young people.

"What we now know is kids who are bullied are about three times more likely to show a range of depressive symptoms than those who aren't. In one of the worst cases, an extortion note was placed in a year 7 Sydney student's locker demanding cash or the student's family would be killed. I've had kids sitting in my room a week after the (bullying) still trembling," he said.

Dr Carr-Gregg said the big challenge for schools was to break the *'thou shalt not dob'* culture. *"I think that many schools are much more alert to this and are trying to put in place some steps,"* he said. But some schools were not taking the issue seriously enough. *"Every school in Australia should have a permanent committee dedicated to looking at this issue."*

Dr Carr-Gregg said, *"An Adelaide computer program, known as the Student relations Assessment Program should be in every school in Victoria - if not Australia. The database allows schools to compare their rates of bullying with other schools."*

Victorian Association of State Secondary Principals president Ted Brierley said bullying was physical and psychological. "Girls are good at this - of cutting people out of the group, making it difficult for them, snide remarks, things like that." Boys were more likely to be the perpetrators of physical bullying. Mr Brierly said, "Most bullying was usually low-grade stuff, so the bully maintains his/her power over someone."

Selecting a school

When selecting a school for your child, avoid any school where there is no anti-bullying policy and especially where the staff or head claims, *"We don't need an anti-bullying policy. There's no bullying here."* It's in these schools that bullying is most prevalent. If the school has an anti-bullying policy, check that it's effective.

The first place to start is by ensuring that every school has an anti-bullying policy that is not only in place - but is enforced. These policies should not only include child bullies, but bullying that involves teachers, school staff and school principals. I believe that the federal government must set a standard for these policies and insist that every school abide by that standard. Laws must be put into place where serious physical and mental bullying by students would be penalised with fines and jail sentences. Some schools have a policy as window-dressing. A policy is only words on paper. Its effectiveness is in the commitment of all school staff to see that it is enforced. Talk to the pupils and ex-pupils in private and in confidence. Talk to the children who are artistic, gifted, of high integrity and non-aggressive - these are the ones most likely to be targeted by bullies.

To find out what a school is really like, ask for the following figures for the last academic year:

Presence of an anti-bullying policy;

- Does that policy include sexual harassment and school hazing?
- What proof is there that they follow that policy?
- Number of student complaints about bullying actions and how these were dealt with;
- Number of expelled students and reasons why they were expelled;
- Number of suicides and attempted suicides amongst pupils;
- Number of suspensions of staff;
- Number of dismissals of staff;
- Number of times the school is involved in employment tribunals or legal action against employees;
- Amount of damage of school property including graffiti.

Profiles of bullies and targets

Bullies: aggressive, physically strong, easily and willingly resorts to violence, poor communication skills, poor social skills, low self-esteem, insecure, may have a dysfunctional home life, thrives on control and dominance, thinks it fun to torment and hurt children who are less physically strong, cowardly, exhibits attention-seeking behaviour and needs to be respected but can't distinguish between *'respect'* and *'fear'*, needs to impress, disrespectful and often contemptuous of others (both children and adults), emotionally and behaviour-ally immature, jealous and envious, divisive and dysfunctional, disruptive, academically below average, often lies, cannot and will not accept responsibility, uncaring, lacks empathy, exploitative.

Targets: physically not as strong as the bully, has a very low propensity to violence and will do everything to avoid resorting to violence to resolve conflict, is artistic, imaginative, creative, academically above average, different (although this is a relative term), caring and empathic, easily forgiving, high integrity, high moral standard, unwilling to resort to lying and deception, often independent, self-reliant, has good relationships with adults, not powerful and eschews classroom politics.

Some people use the words *'swot,' 'isolated'* and *'loner'* to describe targets. I believe these have negative connotations that reinforce notions of *'victim type'*. I prefer the words *'academically a high performer and achiever', 'tends to be independent rather than a socialite'* and *'often prefers to work alone and has no need to impress others.'*

I also prefer the word *'target'* to *'victim'*. The word *'victim'* allows bullies and their supporters to tap into and stimulate people's preconceived notions and prejudices of *'victimhood',* i.e.: that victims are 'weak' and somehow bring the bullying upon themselves. *'Target',* on the other hand, correctly highlights the deliberate act of choice and selection by the bully.

Whilst it is often the target that is regarded as *'weak and inadequate',* it is always the bully who is weak and inadequate - as evidenced by the need to bully. People of strong character and high integrity don't need to bully.

Facts from **'Take Action Against Bullying'** *a manual developed by three Coquitlam, British Columbia, Canada teachers for use in schools, or by parents:*

There are four kinds of bullies:

Physical Bullies: The least sophisticated type of bully. Action-oriented, will hit or kick victims or will take or damage their property. This is the least sophisticated type of bullying because it is so easy to identify. Physical Bullies are soon known to the entire population in the school. As they get older, their attacks usually become more aggressive. These aggressive characteristics manifest themselves as bullies become adults.

Verbal Bullies: Use words to hurt or humiliate another person. This includes name-calling, insulting, making racist comments and constant teasing. This type of bullying is the easiest to inflict on other children. It is quick and to the point. It can occur in the least amount of time available, and its effects can be more devastating in some ways than physical bullying because there are no visible scars.

Relational Bullies: They try to convince their peers to exclude or reject a certain person or people and cut the victims off from their social connections. This type of bullying is linked to verbal bullying and usually occurs when children (most often girls) spread nasty rumours about others or exclude an ex-friend from the peer group. The most devastating effect with this type of bullying is the rejection by the peer group at a time when children most need their social connections.

Reactive Bullies: They straddle a fence of being a bully and/or victim. They are often the most difficult to identify because at first glance, they seem to be targets for other bullies. However, reactive bullies often taunt bullies, and bully other people themselves. Most of the incidents are physical in nature. These victims are impulsive and react quickly to intentional and unintentional physical encounters. In some cases, reactive victims begin as victims and become bullies as they try to retaliate. A reactive victim will approach a person who has been bullying him/her and say something like, *"You better not bug me today, otherwise I'll tell the teacher and boy, will you be in trouble, and so you just better watch out."*

Statements such as this are akin to waving a red flag in front of a raging bull and may provoke a bully into action. They then fight back and claim self-defence.

Sexual Harassment

(This is my own addition to this list)

Very few records have been kept about the number of children who have been sexually harassed at school, but sexual harassment in school is no different than sexual harassment in the workplace. One sexual harassment code states that sexual harassment can include one or more of the following:

- Unwelcome sexual remarks such as jokes, innuendoes, teasing, and verbal abuse;
- Taunts about a person's body, attire, age, sexual preference, marital status;
- Displays of pornographic, offensive or derogatory pictures;
- Practical jokes that cause awkwardness or embarrassment;
- Unwelcome invitations or requests, whether indirect or explicit;
- Intimidation;
- Leering or suggestive gestures;
- Condescension or paternalistic treatment that undermines self-respect;

- Unnecessary physical contact such as touching, patting, pinching, punching or physical assault.

Schools need to include sexual harassment in their anti-bullying policies. Students must understand that sexual comments (including those relating to sexual preference) are not permitted and are a form of bullying. Students and witnesses to sexual harassment would deal with it the same way they would deal with bullying incidents.

Students should also be aware that complaints can be made to their applicable Human Rights Commission or Equal Rights Commission if a school fails in their duty of care and does not stop the behaviour. One sexual harassment law states that:

"Any person responsible for any act of sexual harassment, any supervisor, manager, or person in a position of authority who is aware of the sexual harassment and does not take immediate and appropriate action, (as well as the company) will be named in any complaint brought before the Human Rights Commission."

This means that teachers can no longer *'look the other way'* and pretend that sexual harassment is not occurring. They must step in and stop the harassment; otherwise they too could be charged with sexual harassment because they condoned the behaviour.

Why don't other students help the victim?

They're reluctant to report bullying because they fear retaliation from the bully themselves. Children who are not bullies or victims have a powerful role to play in shaping the behaviour of other children. It's the 60 per cent of children within a school who are not bullied or victimized who hold the key to stop bullying. Children need to be encouraged to speak up on behalf of children they see being bullied. Students who witness bullying have the potential to reduce bullying by refusing to watch bullying, reporting bullying incidents and/or distracting the bully. The key to a successful anti-bullying campaign is to involve everyone in working toward a solution.

The bullying cycle works on witnesses as follows:

- They fear that teachers will confront the bully in such a way that the witnesses are now at risk.
- They fear that their confidentiality will be breached and/or their status within their peer group will be compromised.

Bullies survive by creating the myth that if their behaviour is reported, they will retaliate swiftly and severely. This threat paralyses the victims and witnesses into a code of silence that allows the bully to extend his/her reign of terror.

Unfortunately, many teachers and school staff don't know how to intervene properly, so the bullying continues. This leads to more helplessness for the victims and gives more power to the bullies who know they will get away with their bullying, and/or feel the school has condoned their behaviour.

Teachers need to make it safe for their students to report any bullying incident. They accomplish this by respecting the anonymity of the victim and witnesses. Until the victims and witnesses trust that this will happen -bullying will go unreported, and bullies will be encouraged to continue their actions. Bullies must know the consequences for bullying and schools must consistently enforce the rules. Bullies need counselling, so they can learn how to behave in a socially acceptable manner, as their victims need to learn assertiveness and have confidence that any reported bullying will be dealt with swiftly and effectively by authority figures.

Here's a story one of my friends sent me about a boy who *did* step in to help another student:

"One day, when I was a freshman in high school, I saw a kid from my class walking home from school. His name was Kyle. It looked like he was carrying all his books. I thought to myself, 'Why would anyone bring home all his books on a Friday? He must really be a nerd.'

"I had quite a weekend planned (parties and a football game with my friend's tomorrow afternoon), so I shrugged my shoulders and went on.

"As I was walking, I saw a bunch of kids running toward him. They ran at him, knocking all his books out of his arms and tripping him so he landed in the dirt. His glasses went flying, and I saw them land in the grass about ten feet from him. He looked up and I saw this terrible sadness in his eyes.

"My heart went out to him. So, I jogged over to him and as he crawled around looking for his glasses, and I saw a tear in his eye. As I handed him his glasses, I said, 'Those guys are jerks. They really should get lives.' He looked at me and said, 'Hey thanks!' There was a big smile on his face. It was one of those smiles that showed real gratitude.

"I helped him pick up his books and asked him where he lived. As it turned out, he lived near me, so I asked him why I had never seen him before. He said he had gone to private school before now.

"I would have never hung out with a private school kid before. We talked all the way home, and I carried some of his books. He turned out to be a cool kid. I asked him if he wanted to play a little football with my friends. He said yes. We hung out all weekend and the more I got to know Kyle, the more I liked him, and my friends thought the same of him.

"Monday morning came, and there was Kyle with the huge stack of books again. I stopped him and said, 'Boy, you are gonna really build some serious muscles with this pile of books every day!' He just laughed and handed me half the books.

"Over the next four years, Kyle and I became best friends. When we were seniors, we began to think about college. Kyle decided on Georgetown, and I was going to Duke. I knew that we would always be friends, that the miles would never be a problem. He was going to be a doctor, and I was going for business on a football scholarship.

"Kyle was valedictorian of our class. I teased him all the time about being a nerd. He had to prepare a speech for graduation. "I was so glad it wasn't me having to get up there and speak. Graduation day, I saw Kyle. He looked great. He was one of those guys who really found himself during high school. He filled out and looked good in glasses. He had more dates than I had, and all the girls loved him. Boy, sometimes I was jealous.

"Today was one of those days. I could see that he was nervous about his speech. So, I smacked him on the back and said, 'Hey, big guy, you'll be great!' He looked at me with one of those looks (the grateful one) and smiled. 'Thanks,' he said.

"As he started his speech, he cleared his throat, and began. 'Graduation is a time to thank those who helped you make it through those tough years. Your parents, your teachers, your siblings, maybe a coach...but mostly your friends. I am here to tell all of you that being a friend to someone is the best gift you can give them. I am going to tell you a story.'

"I just looked at my friend with disbelief as he told the story of the first day we met. He had planned to kill himself over the weekend. He talked of how he had cleaned out his locker, so his Mom wouldn't have to do it later and was carrying his stuff home. He looked hard at me and gave me a little smile.

"Thankfully, I was saved. My friend saved me from doing the unspeakable."

"I heard the gasp go through the crowd as this handsome, popular boy told us all about his weakest moment. I saw his Mom and dad looking at me and smiling that same grateful smile. Not until that moment did I realize its depth.

"Never underestimate the power of your actions. With one small gesture you can change a person's life."

As Parents

As soon as their children begin to interact with others, parents need to teach them not to be bullies and how not to be bullied. Teach children the proper words so they can express their feelings. If their pre-schoolers start calling other children names or use unkind words, both parents must intervene immediately and consistently. If they hear comments such as, *"He's not my friend, so he can't share my toys"* the parent must respond with, *"I expect you to share your toys."* Many parents do not know how to intervene in bullying situations, so they overlook the bullying.

Parents need to ask their children if they are being bullied. Whether the child seems to be bullied or not, they should ask them:

"Has anyone bullied you - either going to school or at school? Bullying is different from having fights with your friends, because although fights are unpleasant, they are not as serious."

"If you have been bullied or seen someone else bullied, have you reported it?"

"Is it still ongoing?"

"Why did you not report it to your teacher or at least to us?"

Then follow through with school authorities and don't relent until the bullying has stopped. If the school doesn't have an anti-bullying policy, ask why they don't? Insist that they write and enforce one or move your child to another school.

Children who are repeatedly victimised sometimes see suicide as their only escape. In the UK, at least sixteen children kill themselves each year because of school bullying. This figure is established in the book: **Bullycide: death at playtime.** Each of these deaths is unnecessary, foreseeable, and preventable. Each year 19,000 children attempt suicide in the UK - one every hour.

The incidence of bullying and suicides caused by bullying has risen sharply over the last ten years according to leading children's' charities. Almost half of the children calling the U.K. **ChildLine** in 1999 who were contemplating suicide identified bullying as the main cause. Other pressures included the exam stress and the pressure to score high grades. In 2000 ChildLine received more than 22,000 calls about bullying - making this callers' most prominent problem for the fourth successive year.

A lot of the reported bullying took place on the way to and from school, where schools can argue successfully in court that it's not the school's responsibility. By the DfEE's own admission, over 30 per cent of girls and 25 per cent of boys are afraid to attend school at some time in their life because of bullying. In 1999 **Education Minister David Blunkett** imposed a legal requirement on schools to develop an anti-bullying policy, an instruction that caused every school in the country to divert scarce resources into re-inventing the wheel. The result is that those schools that deal with bullying continue to deal with bullying, whilst those schools who fail in their duty of care now have a piece of paper to wave in court to justify and excuse, often successfully, their denial of responsibility and breach of duty of care.

Many parents don't know their children are being bullied until it's too late. Most bullied children show signs - a lack of vitality, either depression or withdrawal, may be afraid to go to school, or come home missing supplies or possessions. It's a tough call for parents and teachers to make. When is bullying dangerous and when is it child's play? Parents need to keep their eyes and ears open. If a beloved CD player disappears - find out where it went. If money starts disappearing - find out where it's going. If a child is upset after a phone call - s/he's giving you a clue. Follow it. The parents of a loner need to do all they can to help their child find that one true friend, because together, they can more successfully fend off bullies. A child's first interaction with a bully will determine whether that child will be victimised. Body language and level of self-esteem have everything to do with who will be chosen as a target. Bullies pick their prey by first observing the target's body language. Kids need strategies for controlling their body language and dealing with difficult people, just as adults do.

Therefore, parents must instruct their children about what constitutes bullying and insist that they are told immediately if they see or are involved in bullying. It's vital that parents continue the dialogue and they should take the bullying seriously. If they let it go and don't address it - the problem will get bigger.

Is your child a bully?

Here are some signs that your child might be a bully:
- Complaints from school about your child's behaviour;
- Complaints from other parents about your child's behaviour;
- Seems to have unaccountable money;
- Buys things that you know s/he can't afford;
- Explanations that their friends gave them the designer clothes they're wearing;
- Have a cocky, superior air about them.
- Is your child a victim?
- Has trouble sleeping or has lost his/her appetite;
- Crying, depression, sudden rages;
- Is reluctant to go to school - gives excuses that s/he is ill (when you doubt if s/he is);
- Has been in physical fights;
- Comes home from school overly hungry;
- Come home from school with books or clothing torn;
- Asks you to drive him/her to school or changes his/her route to school;
- *'Loses'* things - a sign that someone is stealing the child's items.

School Hazing

Years ago, it was common to have hazing of junior students at the beginning of a school year. Most of the pranks revolved around being the servant of an older student for a day, but lately, that hazing has taken a dangerous turn, and students have been seriously hurt, maimed or even killed when pranks went amiss.

One Canadian student died when the senior students forced their *'slaves'* to consume raw alcohol. One boy was forced to drink a half bottle of vodka until he passed out. When students couldn't revive him, they called for an ambulance. The boy barely survived the ordeal.

***Matthew Voeks*'s** parents pulled him out of his school less than three weeks after he enrolled because of concerns for their son's safety after his teeth and jaw were injured. Older cadets slipped bars of soap inside socks and used them as weapons to beat new cadets. They threw coat hangers at the new cadets and he was repeatedly picked up and slammed to the ground while he was attempting to do push-ups. Voeks said he was injured when an older cadet drill sergeant disciplined him by locking him in a closet. Voeks ran toward the office of a staff member for help, but William Lee Corkins, 17 placed him in a choke hold. He lost consciousness striking his jaw on the floor.

His parents charged Corkins and St. John's Military School in Salina with allegations of hazing. The school denies these allegations. Their suit also alleges the school officially tried to discourage cadets from advising their parents of abusive situations occurring at school and tried to keep the complaints within the chain of command.

Brian Seamons sued his football coach David Snow, and the Cache County School District alleging that his civil rights were violated by the way school officials dealt with the aftermath of hazing by football team mates at Skyview High School. His case took more than seven years to come to trial. A federal judge dismissed it twice, but the rulings were overturned and deemed that Seamons was entitled to a trial.

Seamons alleged that during a school dance his football team mates stripped him of his shorts, bound his hands above his head and tied his hands and feet to a towel rack. He identified five players who had their hands on him. One student hit his genitals with the back of his hand and other students wrapped athletic tape between his legs and up around his neck. While he was tied up and naked, his date for the prom was brought into the locker room. The football players said the incident happened in part to put their team mate *'in his place'*.

The next day Seamons told his father who asked the school to dismiss the five boys from the team. Instead, Snow insisted Seamons not play in a scheduled football game and to take the weekend off to think about reporting the incident. Seamons was eventually suspended and then dismissed from the football team. Former principal Myron Benson said that Seamons was not dismissed from the team but left voluntarily after a heated conversation between football coach Douglas Snow and Seamons' father. James Roe and Chris Griffin both team captains, said all the football players voluntarily signed a written apology a few days after the hazing.

It took the federal jury of five men and six women nearly 12 hours to render its verdict. Seamons was awarded $250,000 in damages. His attorney Dan Larsen said the case wasn't about the actual hazing, but about the football coach's conduct following the incident. It prompted an examination of school hazing policies in the state.

Chapter 4

CASE STUDIES

AUSTRALIA

Ballarat, Victoria

Len Emonson is the father of *Aaron Emonson* who lived through hell - not just through one bullying incident - but for years - and under the eyes of his teachers and other school authorities. This family suffered six years of frustration and pressure. When they'd finally had enough - they sued and won in their case against St. Patrick's College in Ballarat, Victoria.

Len states, *"Our court action could have been avoided had we received supportive action from the principal of St. Patrick's College when we went to him as a last resort, expecting him to take immediate action to protect Aaron and advise us of the action he put in place to achieve this outcome. Unfortunately, he did not see that he had to get involved and stated such under cross examination in court.*

"The year 7 and 8 Co-ordinators saw these boys bullying Aaron, as such a threat to him that they allocated separate home rooms for Aaron and the bullies. This however, did not protect him in other classrooms. Seeing the verbal abuse of Aaron as a problem, the Vice Principal addressed Aaron's class on the matter in early 1997. In mid-1998, a teacher witnessed Aaron punched in the head with such force as to stun the teacher and he wrote a report of the matter to the Vice Principal. However, he did not see the need to send Aaron (an epileptic) to the first aid room or advise us (his parents) of the matter.

"Aaron was punched in the stomach in late 1998 and taken to the first aid room. The Vice Principal called us to pick him up, but no reason was given as to why he was in sick bay or advised of any action taken. We brought up the bullying issue at a support meeting in early 1999 that was noted in the minutes, but no record of any action taken, or feedback was given to us.

"An email was sent from the Co-ordinator to the Vice-Principal in mid-1999 voicing our concern about the continued bullying and that the school should do something. There is no record of any action taken or feedback to us.

"A memo was sent by the welfare officer to the Vice Principal and Co-ordinator that there was a severe problem with bullying of Aaron and some-thing positive needed to be done for Aaron's safety. There is no record of any action taken.

"In September 1999, I contacted Br. Collins about Aaron being attacked in woodworking class with a piece of wood. Br Collins says the incident did not occur, even though a memo was sent to him by a teacher who investigated the matter - testifying to the severe bruising on Aaron's arm.

"I sent an email to Br Collins the first week of November 1999 informing him about Aaron being drenched in one class and having a cord placed around his neck in another, stressing that he take immediate action and to advise me on the action he has taken. Br. Collins in evidence stated he did not see the need for him to get personally involved or contact me on the matter.

"In November 1999, I contacted Br Collins about a threat that Aaron would be receiving a severe beating on the last day of school. No action was taken to ensure Aaron's safety, and Aaron was hit with a blackboard compass in class on the last school day.

"Other facts put forward in the case were; that the school had an anti-bullying policy in place that had been put on all notice boards and read out to every student. However, two boys the school called as witnesses, one a year 12 school captain, had no recollection of seeing it. Also, these same boys stated in court that they did not consider verbal name-calling or abuse as bullying.

"I am convinced that the only reason our case was successful in the courts, was the documentary evidence obtained from the school's files which supported our claim that the bullying occurred, and the school knew of it and took no appropriate action to stop it.

"The biggest weakness in any case parents face in any action they may bring, is the lack of documentary evidence that they have complained about the bullying and the institution they are complaining to - knew of it. By the very nature of things, parents go to their child's teacher to complain of bullying occurring and expect it to be stopped. They at no time expect the bullying to continue over a long period of time, or God forbid, they should find themselves in court because of it, and thereby don't resort to putting their concerns in writing. **A parent's first action on finding their child is being bullied in school is to speak to their child's teacher.** *But if they find they are in the position of doing*

so more than twice, then all future instances should be supported in writing.

Aaron's father was correct when he said, *"It should send a message to all schools that if they have a student like Aaron, they should look out for him and nurture him."* Schools need to focus on treating both the victim and the bully. Aaron left school at the end of Year 10.

Aaron took the Trustees of the Christian Brothers to court for civil damages for personal injuries. Aaron's lawyer, Ballarat solicitor Ron Saines says that Aaron's bullying was at first only verbal, but over the years it became increasingly violent. After deliberating only two and a half hours, the six-person jury awarded Aaron $60,000 in a landmark case which declared that St. Patrick's College breached its duty of care by failing to take adequate steps to deal with his bullying. He stated that the High Court and other courts of authority in Australia and Victoria have ruled repeatedly that the school authority itself is under a clear duty to take reasonable care for the safety of students while they are engaged at school and upon school premises. Documentation showed that St. Patrick's College failed in that duty of care.

Queensland

In March 2002, a 16-year-old Queensland boy decided he had finally *'had enough'* when the ringleader of his bullying, **Aidan Timothy Liyange**, 18 demanded that he give him his CD player, so he could sell it to buy cannabis. The boy fatally stabbed his tormenter in the neck with a kitchen knife as they walked across a football field. His bully and his group of mainly older boys had made the boy's life hell for six months subjecting him to habitual abuse, physical attacks and theft of his property. He accepted the abuse, so he could remain part of the group.

In April 2003, Justice Cate Holmes sentenced the bullied boy to 7 ½ years in jail, part of which he will likely serve in an adult prison. He must serve 70 per cent of his sentence before being eligible to apply for release from prison.

Case Study - from Maroochydore State High School 'Bully Busters' Program (by **Peg Kehret**)

Andrew Buckingham is a bully. He's mean to younger kids and once, when Andrew thought nobody was around, Clancy Schuman saw Andrew kick a little dog. He said when the dog yelped; Andrew laughed and kicked it again.

If there's anything in this world I can't stand, it's a bully. I never did like Andrew Buckingham and after I heard about the dog, I just plain detested him. The problem with bullies is that it's hard to know what to do about them. Most bullies pick out one kid at a time for their victim. Usually, it's a kid who is small for his age or who is somehow different than the other kids. Then the bully harasses that one kid mercilessly.

That's what Andrew did to Clancy. I don't know if it was because Andrew found out that Clancy saw him kick the dog and blabbed it all over the school, or whether he was already picking on Clancy when the dog incident happened. Day after day, Andrew would group to Clancy in the school yard and insult him. If Clancy talked back, Andrew called him a chicken. Either way, Clancy couldn't win. It got so he made excuses not to go out during recess because he knew Andrew would be waiting for him the minute he left the building.

The rest of us watched these proceedings nervously. We felt sorry for Clancy, but we also knew that anyone who intervened would be the next victim. Nobody was eager to claim that honour.

Why didn't Clancy tell the teacher? I guess Clancy thought it was better to get punched around by Andrew than be known as a *'Dobber'*. In our school, dobbing was a sin even worse than bullying.

And one day, Clancy fought back. I don't know why that day was any different than all the days before, but during afternoon recess, Clancy was shooting baskets when Andrew went over to him and announced that he wanted to shoot baskets. Clancy went on dribbling the ball.

"Didn't you hear me, you jerk?" Andrew said. *"I said, it's my turn, so hand over the basketball."*

The minute Andrew raised his voice, a crowd gathered. We all stood in a semi-circle around the side of the basketball court waiting to see what would happen.

Clancy dribbled again, raising his arms and aimed the ball for the basket. It hit the rim and bounced away. Andrew lunged for it, but Clancy was too quick for him. He darted forward, tipped the ball away from Andrew, caught it and dribbled back to the free throw line.

Andrew got red in the face. He swore at Clancy and said he wanted the basketball NOW. Clancy shook his head. Andrew started towards him, his fists clenched, but Clancy stood his ground, clutching that basketball close to his chest. As soon as Andrew was close enough, he socked Clancy's shoulder. Clancy winced, but he didn't let go of the ball. Andrew whacked him again.

My heart was pounding. I didn't want Clancy to give in, but I didn't want to watch him get beat up either.

After Andrew punched him the second time, Clancy set the basketball on the ground next to his feet. Then, without saying a word, he swung his fist at Andrew. Andrew ducked, and Clancy missed him. Andrew's next blow caught Clancy on the cheek and sent him staggering backwards away from the basketball. Andrew leaned forward to pick it up.

That's when I looked around. There were two dozen of us watching and I felt ashamed that none of us would help Clancy. I wasn't eager to have Andrew punch me out, but I knew I couldn't stand there and watch any longer.

As Andrew bent to pick up the basketball, I stepped forward and kicked it out of his reach. I kicked it toward Clancy and if I live to be a thousand, I'll never forget the gratitude in Clancy's eyes as he looked to see who had kicked that ball to him.

I didn't have long to enjoy that look because Andrew started toward me and I could practically see the smoke pouring out of his ears.

"So, you want in the game, do you, loser?" he growled.

I stood next to Clancy, my knees shaking, *"Clancy had the ball,"* I said. *"You have no right to take it away from him."*

I braced myself for the blows that I was sure were coming. And then something extraordinary happened. Two other kids stepped forward, one on either side of me and they told Andrew I was right; that it was Clancy's ball.

As soon as they did that, the rest of the kids surged forward. They gathered around Clancy and me and they all told Andrew to butt off and leave Clancy alone. It was no longer Andrew against Clancy; it was Andrew against the whole year eight class.

Just then, the bell rang. Recess was over, and we had to back inside. It was a relief to sit at my desk. I had been certain I was going to be punched to a pulp and left to die on the basketball court.

Our collective triumph over Andrew exhilarated me, but I kept wondering why we didn't stand up to him sooner. If all of us had stepped in to defend Clancy the first time Andrew picked on him, the whole sorry situation would never have happened. All it took was one show of unity to stop the bully; so why didn't one of us ever suggest to the others that we do t? Why did we let Andrew pick on Clancy all those months? I have no answers. I can only say that I'm glad we finally put a stop to it. Recess is a lot more fun now.

[**Note:** Clancy's rescuer was Opeg Kehret - a girl.]

Melbourne, Victoria

On October 21st, 2002, a 36-year-old man, **Huan Yun Ziang**, a fourth-year commerce student at Monash University went on a shooting rampage with two small pistols killing two and injuring five at Clayton Campus. He carried several handguns and shot indiscriminately. The two dead were **William Wu**, 26 and **Steven Chan**, 26, both honour students in econometrics and business statistics. The injured were, **Laurie Brown, Lee Gordon-Brown, Daniel Urbach, Christine Young** and **Leigh Dat Huynh**. One of the injured had been critically shot in the stomach. The others received injuries to their face, upper body and leg. One woman was shot in the jaw and another had surgery to reattach a finger. Others suffered multiple wounds. His rampage ended when **Bret Inder**, an associate professor of economics, tackled him, one student disarmed him, and several students tackled and held him down. The students then started treating two of the patients.

Monash University Vice chancellor Peter Darvall praised the actions of the *'brave souls'* who wrestled the gun off the attacker. Superintendent Trevor Parks told reporters, *"If he hadn't been tackled, I think we would have had an absolutely tragic circumstance on our hands."*

At a tribute to those killed and injured, Vice-Chancellor Professor Peter Darvall credited the great presence of mind, even heroism, of some of his colleagues. He mentioned Lee Gordon-Brown, **Alistair Boast, Brett Inder** and **Colin Thornby**.

Huan Yun Ziang had permits for his firearms. His classmates and neighbours described him as a quiet man who had problems communicating in English and in court he required the services of a Cantonese translator.

He was charged with two counts of murder and five counts of attempted murder. He faces a maximum sentence of life imprisonment if found guilty of the charges.

Salamander Bay, NSW

April 2003: A 16-year-old boy chased school chased students at Tomaree High School in NSW, and then fired a crossbow arrow from two and a half metres away into his 16-year-old former girlfriend, **Tamara Sharp**'s back. The hunting arrow was sharpened to cause maximum damage. She was critically injured when the arrow passed through her back and chest puncturing her lung and pierced a 16-year-old girl, **Courtney Bennett's** thigh, pinning both her legs. The boy then lit a home-made Molotov cocktail and threw it at Tamara, but even though she was showered with the fuel, it did not explode. He produced a second one and was in the process of lighting it when he was attacked by 16-year-old *Joel Pettit*.

Joel has been hailed a hero when he tackled the youth and averted further tragedy. He had been playing handball with his friends. He saw Tamara covered in blood and her attacker trying to throw a petrol bomb. The bomb didn't ignite. The crossbow-wielding youth tried to burn Pettit with a cigarette lighter just before Joel placed his attacker in a headlock. Then, many students held the attacker until police took him into custody. In the meantime, Joel helped Courtney by keeping her leg elevated to try to stem the bleeding and sat with her until medics arrived. Paramedics had to cut the arrow from Courtney's leg before she could be taken to hospital.

Thankfully Tamara's chest injuries missed all vital blood vessels and organs. One paramedic related, *"It's nothing short of a miracle that this girl (Tamara) survived."*

As many as 100 teenagers may have witnessed the attack. The 16-year-old boy who used the crossbow was taken into police custody and held in Worimi Children's Court. He was charged with attempted murder, two counts of malicious wounding with intent to cause grievous bodily harm, possession of a prohibited weapon and throwing an explosive. Senior Sargeant McInnes said the attack was planned and calculated. The boy had paid $1,084 for his mail-order crossbow and arrows. Magistrate Jane Motle refused bail and remanded him in custody until April 28, 2003.

The attacker is described as a loner who was not very popular but was a good student who came from a loving and solid family.

Letters from bullied children

"My name is Chris and I come from an okay family. My problems at school. A group of guys are giving me a really hard time. They call me a loser - they call me other names, but I don't want to talk about that. They're giving me a hard time all the time. Things like hiding my school bag at lunch time, tripping me up and stopping me from getting onto the basketball courts. I've got some friends, but they're not always around when I need them. It's really getting to me. Anyway, yesterday I couldn't stand it any longer - I got stuck into one of those guys. Everyone crowded around for the fight. I'm on three days suspension.

Teachers have noticed that I'm not 'paying attention in class'. That's because I'm thinking about what they might do next."

"Hi, my name is Amy. I really like school... NOT. I'm quite good at most subjects and like my netball. Things started to go bad for me when Jane came. She wanted to join our group. At first, I thought Jane was my friend, but then she took my best friend Becky and started to turn my friends against me. I found a nasty note that she wrote to my ex best friend about me! Why do they believe her? The only one being nice to me is Kate, but she's not really in the group. I sit by myself or with her at lunch times. I feel like such a loner. I cry myself to sleep at night. My parents are always in a bad mood with me, because I get mad at my sister all the time."

Chapter 5

CASE STUDIES

UNITED KINGDOM

U.K. Case Studies - **Information supplied by Tim Field of BullyOnline** www.bullyonline.org (who publishes a monthly newsletter with items on workplace bullying, school bullying, stress, PTSD and psychiatric injury.)

In April 1998, 14-year-old **Brian Franklish** died while trying to escape the children bullying him. He was killed escaping a school bully gang on a friend's motorbike.

Yorkshire: Twelve-year-old **Debbie Shaw** agreed to a challenge by other girls to end her victimisation by fighting her school bully. She died of her injuries.

Thirteen-year-old **Roger Hillyard** was found dead near his home after a lifetime of bullying

Sisters **Samantha and Michaela Kendal** were so taunted about being overweight that they went on hunger strike ... both died

Burton-Upon-Trent: Fifteen-year-old choirboy **Darren Steele** was found hanged in his bedroom after a life of victimisation at school. Darren's mother found him hanging in his bedroom the day he had run away from a group of pupils after school. 15-year-old Darren was teased and called *'gay boy'* and *'poof'* because he loved to cook and took drama lessons. One schoolmate said she'd seen Darren's school bag, back and head burned with cigarettes

September 1997 - 13-year-old **Kelly Yeomans** committed suicide after being bullied at school. Five boys who tormented the Derby teenager were ordered to spend time at an attendance centre.

West Midlands: Twelve-year-old schoolboy **Stephen Woodhall** hanged himself with his brother's school tie rather than face school bullies for another day. *"He must have been going through hell,"* his father, Ken, said. Later, forty-seven-year-old **Kenneth Woodhall** also hanged himself. He had never got over the hanging suicide five years earlier of his son Stephen.

Stephen Sandon, six, collapsed and died in terror of a bully pack almost a year to the day after the death of **Joanna Canlin** in the same tough schoolyard.

Isle of Lewis: Fifteen-year-old **Marianne Bisenieks** died of an overdose. She is said to have been bullied at the same school as sixteen-year-old **Katherine Jane Morrison** who took an overdose in 1996. Two schoolgirls were jailed for Katherine's death.

Ireland: fourteen-year-old **Kurt Cobain** shot himself to escape the local bullyboys.

1997, **Vijay Singh Shahiri** hanged himself after writing heartbreaking poems about his schoolyard tormentors. Entries in his diary included *"Monday: My money was taken. Tuesday: names called. Wednesday: Uniform torn. Thursday: My body pouring with blood. Friday: It's ended. Saturday: Freedom."* Vijay was found hanging from the banister of his home by a silk scarf on Saturday.

Fourteen-year-old **Amanda Brownridge** overdosed because of bullying.

Schoolgirl dancer **Kelly Farrar**, 13, killed herself with her father's heart pills after telling friends she'd been teased at school.

Surrey: **Mark MacLaglan** hanged himself from a tree because of bullying.

Abingdon, Oxfordshire: Teenage cyclist **Mark Perry** risked the road to escape a gang of bullies. He died under the wheels of a truck. Mark's death lead to the setting up of the Anti-Bullying Campaign.

Kent: Child prodigy **James Lambeth**, 16, who was bullied because of his genius, gassed himself in his father's car.

An un-named Asian boy was knifed to death in a suicidal bid to stand up against the bullies who had made his life hell.

London: Eleven-year-old **Martin Harvey**, a long-time victim, collapsed and died when a bully gang charged him in the playground.

Cheshire: **Mark Harvey**, 15, was beaten by a bully gang outside school and died after refusing to run away.

Surrey: **Peter Evans**, 11, was crushed under the wheels of a lorry while trying to escape a bully gang.

Hampshire: Fourteen-year-old **Tom Brough** hanged himself. Witnesses at his inquest admitted to having been part of a bully campaign against him.

Six-year-old ***Matthew Bibby*** risked the busy rush hour road rather than his bullies and was killed by a car as he tries to escape them.

Mid-Glamorgan: ***Jamie Evans***, 14, hanged himself with his belt after long-term school bullying culminated in the shaving off one of his eyebrows.

Scotland: ***Suzie Barclay*** took an overdose of pills after vicious playground taunts ... five months after another girl at her school narrowly escaped an overdose death to end her own bully torment.

Fife: ***George Goodall***, 13, was killed by a police car as he dashed across a road to escape pursuing bullies. Just a week before George Goodall's death, 12-year-old ***Michael Gourley***, was bullied into playing chicken on a busy motorway. He was also run over and killed by a police car.

Ayrshire: Fifteen-year-old ***Peter Sinclair*** fell through the ice and died. He was playing truant to avoid bullies. His mother forgave the bullies and invited them to his funeral.

Seven-stone ***Daniel Mole*** was chased and beaten by the thug who had bullied him throughout his school life. He died falling from a roof attempting to escape. It was his 21st birthday.

Lanarkshire: A 12-year-old pupil at a top fee-paying school hanged himself from a tree to escape merciless bullying.

Wales: ***Jemma Brine-Daniels***, 14, died of an overdose after being bullied at school... by teachers.

Alistair Hunter, aged 12, hanged himself after a campaign of bullying which involved him being spat upon and bullies urinating in his sports bag.

Nine-year-old ***Neil Gadd*** chose the main road, rather than face bullies blocking the subway pass. He was knocked down and killed.

Merthyr Tydfill, South Wales: ***Anthony Hutchinson*** jumped off a window ledge and later died in his bedroom after being bullied by other pupils because he was coloured.

May 2000: 15-year-old ***Gail Jones*** from Tranmere, Merseyside, took an overdose of paracetamol after a long campaign of bullying, harassment and threats via her mobile phone. Within half an hour she received twenty abusive messages.

14 February 2001: 10-year-old ***Jevan Richardson*** hanged himself at his home in Lewisham yesterday after being expelled from St Mary

Magdelene's Catholic Primary School, Brockley. In a suicide note, Jevan wrote *"I can't get anything right. I'm always wrong. I just want to die and I'm going to hang myself."*

Lewisham Council have refused to comment. Chair of governors Don Mahony raised doubts about the competency of head teacher Carmelita Winston when he wrote to Jevan's parents stating that the presence of their son at the school was "Damaging to the health and welfare of the head teacher Carmelita Winston." This statement also calls into question Ms Winston's suitability for the post of headmistress and the fact that she does not have control of discipline at St Mary Magdelene's Catholic Primary School. Ms Winston's (white) long-running battle with Jevan and his parents (black) is more indicative of a vendetta against the family. Teachers and lecturers are the largest group of callers to the UK National Workplace Bullying Advice Line; in most cases the reported bully is the head teacher with the behaviour profile of a serial bully.

7 March 2001: 13-year-old **Kayleigh Davies** hanged herself in her bedroom on 20 December 2000. Her father, Martin Davies, found her hanging in her bedroom. Central Hampshire coroner Grahame Short recorded a verdict of suicide after hearing how Kayleigh had been sent home from Alderman Quilley School in the morning of the last day of term by headmaster Kenneth Button for drinking alcohol. Mr Dawes told the coroner that because of bullying, Kayleigh had been moved from Crestwood School in Eastleigh to nearby Alderman Quilley where, after an initial period of calm, experienced bullying again. The inquest heard how it appeared Kayleigh had been thinking of suicide for some time and became intensely interested in rap music, especially Eminem, and pop stars like Jim Morrison who had gone out early.

23 June 2001: **Nicola Raphael**, 15, died after taking an overdose of painkillers at her home in Kirkintilloch, Dunbartonshire, Scotland. She had been the target of bullying for some time. The bullies at Lenzie Academy had speciously used her style of dress - which they labelled *'Gothic'* - as a rationalisation for their violence towards her and had branded her *'a freak'*.

A spokeswoman for East Dunbartonshire Council said that *"Nicola was part of a group within the school which received unwanted attention from other pupils and where incidents were reported, and names provided, investigations were carried out and appropriate action taken."*

Lenzie Academy appears to be a school obsessed with ensuring children wear the correct school uniform, but that obsession doesn't extend to its duty of care

[**Note:** Tim Field] Any person in a position of power who is obsessed with controlling what children wear, especially in respect of school uniform, needs to be regarded as a potential abuser. If this includes controlling the colour of underwear, the person needs to be regarded as a potential sexual abuser.)

21 November 2001: an inquest was opened into the suicide of 13-year-old Nottingham teenager **Morgan Musson**. On 15 November 2001, she took 40 tablets of the painkiller Coproxamol, went to bed and was found by her mother, Debra Savage the next morning. Debra claimed that her daughter had been taunted and bullied by girls from Ellis Guilford School in Nottingham for seven months. (Morgan was 6ft tall). She felt the school had not done enough to deal with the bullying.

Even though her parents moved her to another school, the bullying continued because the gang lived nearby. Mrs. Savage blames the school and the bullies for her daughter's death. Nottingham LEA said they had acted but there was no evidence to suggest that the bullying amounted to anything more than verbal abuse. Ellis Guilford headmaster Peter Plummer declined to comment.

Update 20 February 2002: the inquest on 13-year-old Morgan Musson has returned an open verdict as the coroner could not satisfy himself that she intended to kill herself. Unlike a physical injury or physical cause of death, a psychiatric injury cannot be studied and recorded after death. All the coroner has is (sometimes) the suicide letter and (always) the denial of everyone who contributed to the bullycide: the bullies, the witnesses of bullying, and those in authority who should have acted, but didn't. Greater weight is often attached to these denials than to the written and reported testimony of the deceased who has been tormented to death and to the deceased's family who have lived (and continue to live) the nightmare. An open verdict, which may be legally correct, neither relieves the suffering of the family nor does it enable the perpetrators to be held accountable for their sins of commission and omission.

In April 2002, **Laura Kilibarda** 13 was found by her mother hanging by a strip of cloth from the rafters in her bedroom at the family home in Lisvane, near Cardiff. Laura, a member of a riding club in Cardiff, was seen walking her dog through Lisvane two hours before she died.

She was a year-eight pupil at the 1,500-pupil Llanishen High School in Cardiff, where she was said to have been doing well.

During an inquest into her death on October 23, 2002, police said they found no evidence that Laura had been the victim of a bullying campaign. However, Laura's parents, George and Penny Kilibarda said that their daughter's friends stated she had been targeted. Laura would never point the finger at anyone. Her mother said, *"When asked about bullying Laura said, 'I try and avoid people that could be aggressive, I try and stay with my friends,' that was her way of dealing with it."* Following the hearing, Penny said: *"There must be somebody that she talked to; someone must have the knowledge that she was planning what she was doing."*

At the inquest, her GP explained that Laura had visited him two days before her death asking for a pregnancy test. The test was negative. She also showed him self-inflicted cuts on her arms and stomach

Detective Constable Michael Hicks said: *"She kept it (diary) for six-months up until a fortnight before her death, and a torn-up note revealed she had suicidal thoughts. There were a lot of sad undertones. She was clearly unhappy and made certain comments - one said that she was considering killing herself."* Cardiff and Vale Coroner Doctor Lawrence Addicott recorded a suicide verdict.

11 September 2002: 12-year-old **Emma Morrison** was found hanging in the bedroom of her Edinburgh home after being subjected to a campaign of verbal and physical abuse by school bullies at Broughton High School. She had been called names and hit with school supplies such as pencils and rubbers by a gang of girls. They called her *'ugly'*, and *'pizza face'* because of her acne. The only one she confided in about her bullying was her mother, who was separated from the father. Emma had a good relationship with her father. Her grandfather accused the school of acting like ostriches, burying their heads in the sand. Emma had stayed home from school for two weeks before her death to escape the continual teasing. The education authority said it was not aware of any evidence of bullying.

Her mother found Emma was in her bedroom that morning. She had left notes for her mother and a girlfriend.

In December 2001, 14-year-old **Scott Young** died of multiple injuries after being struck by two cars. He ran away to escape a bully but in doing so, ran into the road to his death. **Yannick Etutu**, 17 of Ilford, East London, who punched and chased him, was jailed for three years for manslaughter.

August 2002, 13-year-old ***Jack Glasby*** hung himself after being bullied at Caedmon School, Whitby, Yorkshire, which he had left five months previously. As a study by Kidscape found, the cumulative psychiatric injury caused by bullying at school endures, often throughout life. Problems for Glasby started in February 2001, when another pupil hung him over a stairwell and said he would drop him. Caedmon School head teacher Tony Hewitt told the inquest that the school offered strategies to help Jack and stressed that all incidents of bullying - however minor - were dealt with and documented.

Following a series of physical attacks, a Carmarthen schoolgirl from Llansteffan ended up slashing her wrists with a compass in a cry for help because teachers couldn't protect her from months of bullying. Things became worse for her when the bullies were identified.

20 September 2001: 14-year-old **Laura Grimes** committed suicide by taking an overdose of painkillers after being bullied at school and rejected by friends.

Laura took a massive overdose of Co-proxamol painkillers after leaving eleven suicide notes. Headmaster of Mangotsfield School, Derek Hall, said that the school had a very strict policy on bullying, and that Laura had never complained of bullying to her tutor, head of year or to her large number of friends. In his statement, Derek Hall said her death had caused much upset and grief. *"Laura always seemed a happy and contented girl at school,"* he said. *"If any parent phones in, reporting that their son or daughter is being bullied, it is thoroughly investigated, and a record is kept. We received no such call from Mrs Grimes. We have a trained counsellor on site and we have individual and group mentoring on a regular basis."* Laura had not told her parents of her ordeal (the reasons why children do this are revealed in ***Bullycide: death at playtime***).

Laura had planned her own funeral and even left a will before killing herself. Laura Grimes' parents have decided to publicise the collection of documents and letters they discovered after her death. The full impact of the letters had not been revealed to them until after an inquest into the teenager's death. It read: *"Don't worry about me, I have gone up above where I really want to be, no bullies, no school, just happiness."* Another letter intended for the bullies themselves warned them that they *"should never pick on anyone else"*.

Before her suicide in July 2001, Laura had been looking forward to being a bridesmaid at her sister's wedding. She had been popular with a close circle of friends and her parents had no idea of what was happening to her. Her mother Susan Grimes said: *"There were absolutely no outward signs at all. It is very difficult to detect. She comes from a very close family and nobody in the family had any idea at all. We did not know why it had happened until after the inquest when all the letters and the pile of documents that she had left were passed on to us. It was a tremendous shock. "I don't think anyone can understand what it is like going in at 0700 to call your daughter for school and finding that she is dead."*

On 20 September 2001 the Avon and District coroner Paul Forrest recorded a verdict of suicide. In her hand written will Laura told people to *'live a normal life'* after her departure.

[Note: Tim Field]: Head of Queen Elizabeth Maridunum School, Mr Gwyn Thomas claimed that the school took bullying very seriously. Displaying his lack of knowledge of the need to be proactive not reactive, Mr Thomas denied responsibility by saying that, *"Unfortunately, if we are not made aware of allegations in any way, there is little we can do. We also promote Childline services in the school and are very proactive on preventing this kind of thing."* If a child is in the position of having to contact Childline, has not the school already failed in its anti-bullying policy and in its duty of care?

ChildLine

ChildLine reported in November 1999 that it had received its one millionth call since its inception in 1986. About a quarter of all calls were from children suffering abuse and violence, often at the hands of parents or family members. ChildLine's findings show that children as young as six feel suicidal. The main reasons are bullying, abuse, and exam stress. At least 500 calls to ChildLine each year are from children who will attempt suicide. Even more shocking is that the psychiatric injury caused by bullying, abuse and exam stress results in hundreds of young adults committing suicide after they leave school; in 1998 - 571 young men and 159 young women aged 15 to 24 killed themselves.

27 November 2001: fifteen-year-old **Elaine Swift** died from an overdose of painkillers after a campaign of bullying, harassment and assault that started after she was featured in the media for having donated bone marrow to her younger sister who was suffering from leukaemia. Elaine's parents say that they were let down by the LEA who failed to take her allegations seriously. The bullying comprised

daily verbal harassment and taunting, and on one occasion a lighted match was thrown into her hair, which caught fire. The situation had become so untenable that Elaine was moved from Brierton School in Hartlepool last year.

Head teacher of Brierton School Stuart Priestley stated that his school had a *'rigorous anti-bullying policy'* and that every incident of bullying that was reported was investigated. Bill Jordon, head teacher at Elaine's new school, Dyke House in Hartlepool, said that he was satisfied with steps taken to deal with the bullying claims made by Elaine. Hartlepool's assistant director of education Adrienne Simcock asserted, *"I am confident that the school has acted properly and taken all the appropriate steps when investigating the claims."*

Elaine died after an emergency liver transplant failed to reverse the effects of 100 paracetamol tablets taken over a period of a fortnight.

2000 - 2002: 12-year-old potential Olympic skating champion *Aaron Vays* endured physical and verbal abuse from fellow students. When he stood up for himself at school in the absence of the school taking effective action, he was further victimised by the school principal.

[Tim Field adds: In schools where bullying is rife, it's usually because the principal does not have control of discipline].

While in pursuit of his Olympic skating dream, Aaron endured physical and verbal abuse from fellow students, simply because he's a boy who likes to skate. He began figure skating at age 5 after his parents moved from the Ukraine to United States.

Two years ago, when he was in the fifth grade and proud of his second-place finish in a competition, Aaron took his trophy to Haverstraw Middle School to show his principal, but another student destroyed it. His parents, Boris and Polina Vays, say the cruelty didn't stop with words. The abuse turned personal and physical last November. Teasing and taunting turned into punching and tripping. One bully beat and kicked Aaron while another student held him down, the boy said. *"I got kicked in the rectum and it hurt so much, I had a bowel movement at that time,"* Aaron revealed on television on the *Good Morning America* program. The boy suffered internal injuries in that incident, his parents said.

His mother Polina said she didn't report the incident because she had no idea what was going on until months later when nightmares sent her son racing into her bedroom. Aaron moved to Willow Grove

Middle School. *"They transferred him,"* said Boris Vays, *"They punished him, instead of the kids who did this."*

Aaron kept skating, but says he kept quiet - trying to avoid any further trouble. Then in April 2002, some hockey players spotted him at the rink where he practices two hours a day, six days a week and bullied him again. The injuries made Aaron and his parents realise it was time to fight back, they said. This time, his parents filed a police complaint and began legal action against the North Rockland District charging that school officials failed to protect their son and gathered publicity for their case.

"We weren't interested in this lawsuit," said his father. *"We tried five or six times to speak to the school district, to get them to help out. We didn't report things to the police. Nothing happened. Things got worse and worse. We had no choice."* The Vays say they are just looking for a community where their son's achievements, including a 10th-place finish at the nationals last year, will be appreciated, even celebrated. *"I'd like to skate for the United States in the Olympics in 2006,"* Aaron Vays said. *"And I'd like this to stop. I don't want anyone to go through this. I want to have a good social life, to have a good, normal life."*

April 18, 2002: 14-year-old **Adam Grigg** hanged himself with a lanyard from his sea cadet's uniform after three years of bullying that started at Broadgate Primary School, Horsforth, Leeds, and continued when he moved to Horsforth School. Adam was described as a quiet, sensitive child who loved to play with computers and his pet dog. He was looking forward to a career in the Royal Navy. Instead, he endured three years of being spat upon, beaten up, and had threatening notes written in his school books - which culminated in his suicide to escape the violence.

An inquest on 15-year-old **Hannah Taylerson** has returned a verdict of *'self-harm'*. Hannah hanged herself with her school tie after having problems at school that included peers talking about her behind her back. Hannah was found by her mother Diane hanging between clothes in the wardrobe.

Previously Hannah had visited her doctor with self-inflicted cuts that she told him were due to problems at her school (John Cabot City Technology College in Bristol, England). It makes one wonder why her physician didn't take more direct action to avert this tragedy. In addition, Hannah had recently visited school counsellors, but had apparently not told them about the bullying. Her mother, Diane, said after the hearing that the family had no idea Hannah felt so desperate.

A friend told the Bristol inquest that the teenager was upset by gossip at John Cabot City Technology College in Kingswood, and about splitting up with her boyfriend. Hannah told her friend Emily Peters she wanted to kill herself. However, on a shopping trip, days before her death, she had told Emily she had sought counselling at school and seemed happy. Hannah had not told school counsellors about the severity of her problems, the inquest heard.

In a statement read to the court Mrs Taylerson said she had heard music coming from the bedroom but got no reply as she knocked on the door and tried to get her daughter's attention by switching the electricity supply on and off. Eventually she went in and found Hannah in the wardrobe, hanging from the clothes rail.

Bristol coroner Paul Forrest said: *"This girl had problems with friends and her boyfriend and she took her own life."*

13-year-old **Amie Salmon** was withdrawn from Glaisdale Comprehensive in Bilborough, Nottingham, after a year of bullying. Instead of dealing with the bullies, Amie was thrust into the spotlight by being given a mobile phone and special access to her teacher - which accentuated the victimisation rather than dealt with the cause. The school's head teacher says he has found it difficult to get at the facts of the case - but after a year appears still not to have undertaken any training on the subject.

Leah Bradford-Smart, 21 lost her case for damages for persistent and prolonged bullying that occurred when she was a pupil at Ifield Middle School, Crawley, West Susses between 1990 and 1993. In a ruling in the High Court Mr Justice Garland said that, *"Although a school might know that a pupil was being bullied at home or on the way to school, teachers only owed a duty to prevent the behaviour spilling over into the school. Her treatment by fellow pupils inside school was not severe nor prolonged enough to merit calling it bullying."* Miss Bradford-Smart says she was branded by pupils as an exhibitionist and a prostitute who flaunted her body. They had seen her in a paddling pool at home with just her knickers on. She said she was chased around the playground, thrown against fences, suffered taunts, and on one occasion was pushed onto a road in front of a car while she was waiting for the school bus.

West Sussex County Council argued successfully that there was very little sign that she was being bullied while at school, and that the education authority could not be responsible for behaviour outside school. Despite this harassment and assault (which if she were an adult might result in charges of attempted murder) she still managed to perform well at school, so the school was able to argue that her performance was not affected and thus the bullying was not severe enough to merit a claim for damages.

The appeal judges said that there may be occasions when a school was in breach of its duty to combat bullying even if it was outside school, but *"these occasions will be few and far between"*.

4 April 2000: 10-year-old **Louise Beal** has returned to Launcelot Primary School in Lewisham, south-east London, after teachers were assigned as her bodyguards to protect her from bullying. However, as with Amie Salmon, such action drew attention to the victimhood of the target rather than tackled the source of the problem. The bullies were probably enjoying the gratification that came from the power of seeing adults forced to take extreme measures due to their behaviour.

[**Note:** Tim Field] In several cases reported to the UK National Workplace Bullying advice line involving teachers being bullied, those responsible for bullying do not have control of discipline and can only maintain control through fear and threat. In such schools, bullying is rife amongst both adults and children. These are also often the schools that, when asked about bullying, reply with *"We don't have bullying here. It's not a problem."* These schools simply do not understand that the behaviour they are observing every day is bullying and abusive.

Another case involving a ten-year-old was the murder of **Damilola Taylor**. Damilola was stabbed on the way home from Oliver Goldsmith Primary School in Peckham, London. He bled to death in a stairwell after an artery in his leg was severed. Before any substantive evidence had been released, the headmaster of Oliver Goldsmith Primary school, Mark Parsons, immediately denied any connection between Damilola's death and bullying at his school which he said was *'limited to name-calling and playground scuffles.'* Damilola's mother had been to the school the previous day to complain of bullying.

Daniel Overfield hanged himself after a teacher told him he had *'the attention span of a goldfish'*. The coroner recorded a verdict of misadventure as he believed Daniel probably did not intend to kill himself.

[**Note:** Tim Field] Sarcasm appears frequently in bullying cases as it is a device whose intention is to hurt; many do not know this and thus use it unwittingly. Reading between the lines, Daniel had already suffered psychiatric injury, possibly from bullying and this remark, although not particularly devastating, was the final straw. Daniel's case also reveals the bullying nature of an education system that forces children to undertake subjects of dubious relevance in which they have no interest and then punishes them for not excelling.

14 April 2000, ***Denise Bailie***, 14, of Belfast Model School for Girls, committed suicide because of bullying.

Flora Harman, the mother of ***Jacob Harman*** intends to sue the Superintendent of Schools, Anthony J. Perrelli, the Board of Education and the town because she and her son have suffered emotional and physical injuries from repeated bullying her son received while he was riding the school bus.

In 2000 Jacob twice suffered injuries when another student attacked him while he was riding in a town school bus. The next year he was attacked again by the same student - again suffering injuries. Perrelli offered the boy alternate transportation either in a separate van or through reassignment to a different school bus. The bully was allowed to continue taking his usual school bus, because he was on medication and had received counselling.

SCOTLAND

Natalie King, 13 in the first case of its kind in Scotland, is suing the Aberdeen City Council for up to £20,000 for the psychological damage she suffered because of the alleged bullying she claims the school and local authority did nothing to prevent. She was bullied between March and September of 2001, that included being elbowed in the stomach, kicked in the leg and had coins thrown at her. The verbal abuse included calling her a *'slag,' 'slut', 'whore,'* and *'bitch'* and thee pupils had threatened to kill her.

Even though she reported the incidents to the school, the school did nothing. Aberdeen City Council denies that it has been negligent. A spokeswoman said, *"We have a long-standing anti-bullying policy in place. Allegations of bullying are taken very seriously, and school have measures in place to deal with any such allegations."*

Debra Scott was so traumatised by ongoing physical and verbal abuse that after one school episode she went home crying, took a bunch of her mother's tablets, trying to kill herself. Her Mom got home a couple of hours later and Debra told her what had happened, and she received treatment. She was away from school for about a week. The bullying stopped for a year, and then the teasing began again. Kids didn't speak to her because she'd dobbed on the boys earlier. Other girls tied her shoelaces together and pushed her down on the grass and ripped off her t-shirt and bras, holding her arms open so that her breasts were fully visible to nearby boys. On her way home from school the same day, another girl poured spaghetti over her head.

It reached a point where Debra refused to go to school and her parents began legal action. Unfortunately, her parents had not documented the cases of bullying on paper so there was backup evidence they could produce to prove bullying. Unfortunately, Debra lost her case against the school.

[**Note:** Tim Field: Let this be a warning to parents that they must put their concerns about the bullying of their children in writing and ask for written reports on how the school dealt with their bullying complaint. To win a case in court, it must appear that the school knew about the bullying and did little or nothing to deal with it.]

A gentle giant was killed trying to protect four schoolgirls from a 30-strong mob. **Christian Smith,** 24 was repeatedly knifed and beaten by a gang of teenage bullies outside his home. They set upon the 6 ft 4 in dad-of-one, who died in hospital. The mother of one of the young girls said, *"I owe my child's life to him. He has died a hero in my book."* The 15-year-old was one of four girls approached by a group of about seven youths outside Christian's home in the Littlemoor area of Oldham. The girl said: *"One recognised me. They started threatening me. Christian was watching from the doorstep. I had only known him four days, but he had experienced bullying himself and he stuck up for us. He was just like a big, cuddly teddy bear."*

But the gang returned later with reinforcements and attacked Christian, who was trying to make them back off with a sword. The girl said: *"There were too many for anyone to handle. It was obvious he was dead. If it wasn't him, it'd have been me."*

Christian's mum, Christine, said: *"How am I going to explain this to his three-year-old son that he will not see him again."*

Daniel Nield, 18 of Oldham, has been charged with violent disorder. Four others are being questioned. (Steve Purcell of the Daily Mirror)

Chapter 6

CASE STUDIES

CANADA

Mission, British Columbia

Mission, B.C. (just east of Vancouver) - In a March 2002 court case, Police charged two girls with uttering threats in connection with the suicide of a 14-year-old girl. One of them was also accused of criminal harassment. A teenager who bullied her into committing suicide has been found guilty of uttering threats and criminal harassment. A second accused was found not guilty at the landmark trial in British Columbia. Their identities are protected because they were prosecuted under Canada's Young Offenders Act. The 16-year-old who was found guilty of both charges underwent four to six weeks of assessments before a judge-imposed sentence.

Dawn-Marie Wesley's younger brother found her in her bedroom where she had hanged herself with a dog leash on November 10, 2000 after talking on the phone with girls who bullied her. She left a suicide note naming three girls at her school she said were *'killing her'* because of their bullying. *"If I try to get help, it will get worse. They are always looking for a new person to beat up, and they are the toughest girls. If I ratted, they would get suspended and there would be no stopping them. I love you all so much."* Police say the Crown is reviewing their recommendations to charge two 15-year-old girls with uttering threats. One girl is the daughter of an RCMP officer. The girls named in the suicide note have been suspended from school.

Parents and students at Mission Secondary school talked about school bullying and suicide prevention. They're concerned the school's *'zero tolerance'* policy for bullying did not prevent Dawn-Marie's death.

The child's mother, Cindy Wesley said, *"This wasn't just for Dawn-Marie today. This ruling goes for every child in this country that's been bullied. I think you need to acknowledge that although our family was the major victim in all of this, our community was a victim, the high school was a victim, and the families of those girls are victims of their own children."*

In her ruling, B.C. Provincial Court Judge Jill Rounthwaite said that it was clear that one of the accused had bullied Wesley repeatedly, giving the victim reason to fear for her life. Although the second accused had taken part in the phone call, the judge said there was no evidence the girl had broken the law.

Rounthwaite noted that bystanders added *'to the power of the bully'* by letting the harassment go on without intervening. *"None of those people had the moral strength to tell the bully to stop or go away,"* the judge said.

Halifax, Nova Scotia

In April 2002, **Emmet Fralick**, a 14-year-old grade 9 student at St. Agnes School in Halifax, Nova Scotia, shot himself in his bedroom because he was being bullied by classmates. It's not clear how the teen obtained the gun. He left behind a suicide note and poem that said he could no longer endure being bullied. He did not name names. Emmet was regarded as a quiet boy with a reputation for kindness to others.

The boy's death came less than two weeks after the high-profile trial of two girls in British Columbia who were charged with bullying a former friend and causing her suicide. One was acquitted; the other found guilty of criminal harassment and uttering threats.

Nova Scotia is considered a leader in anti-bullying strategies, and the home province for programs initiated by the League of Peaceful Schools. St. Agnes has conducted anti-bullying presentations and has a race-relations officer.

Police first learned of the bullying allegations when a community officer went to the school to help the school's 320 students deal with the grief of their classmates' suicide. While there, she was told several times that Fralick had been the target of bullying. Rumours alleged that Fralick had been bullied by a gang led by a girl who routinely demanded money from other students, forcing some to resort to shoplifting so they could pay her. The principal, Charles O'Hanley said there were no signs or reports that Fralick had been bullied, and he would have expected Fralick, a former peer counsellor, to report it. He had no obvious evidence that he was in distress. Fralick's death was hard for the teachers to deal with because they felt they didn't recognise that he was at risk.

As the shock subsided, the student's angry reaction began against the alleged bully. The 15-year-old Halifax girl suspected of bullying Emmet before he committed suicide has a lengthy criminal record with over 20 convictions for assaults and theft. She was convicted in July with four counts of extortion two counts of assault and one count of threats related to the case.

When she started school, she cut her shoulder-length hair and began dressing like a boy. She got into fights with boys, but never picked on girls. In one of those fights, Fralick ended up with two black eyes. The girl chose Fralick to pick on because he didn't fight back (he wouldn't fight a girl). She said she had nothing against him, but he'd steal for her. Some students claim she extorted up to $80 a day from Fralick, who had to resort to shoplifting to pay her for fear of being beaten. Fralick was picked up for shoplifting at Sears in Halifax Shopping Centre the month before his suicide but was not charged. The group of students threatened workers and clerks working in the mall which is right across the street from St. Agnes.

The bully's mother defended her daughter saying, *"She's a good girl,"* and she added that, *"She felt like a prisoner in her own home."* The Fralick home is close to theirs and everyone in the neighbourhood talked about the allegations. One neighbour was overheard saying, *"She did it. She's a thief and a liar. They should put the little bitch in jail."*

The principal called the mother to explain that a school board meeting had determined that her daughter was no longer welcome at the school. The girl urged her mother to leave town.

Students alleged she headed the gang that extorted money from students. One girl who knew Emmet said, *"If we had told, she would have got Emmet worse. If they put her away, her friends would just take over."*

Another parent acknowledged that her own son was also bullied at the school. *"He went through hell for three weeks. It was brutal."* He said his son and other students have been intimidated by larger classmates, who slam them into lockers in the halls and chant abusive phrases at them in the school yard. Earlier that year the father went to the school and contacted the school board, threatening to turn to the media if nothing was done to help his boy. The school called in a mediator. It appeared that school officials were being intimidated too. He believes that they should have done something, instead of being concerned that somebody might slice the tires on their cars.

Education Minister Jane Purves revealed that a member of her family was also a victim of the same girl. One of her young relatives was bullied the summer before. She refused to identify the relative for fear of putting that person in danger. It's frightening to realise that even a junior high school bully could scare such a person as the head of the province's public-school system.

She will be establishing a province-wide database of bullies, so the schools can track violent students. The system will use a system being used by Cape Breton-Victoria Regional School Board that monitors student suspensions and expulsions. This data gives educators a better idea about the amount and degree of aggressive behaviour in schools. It would also draw attention to situations where suspensions were given for relatively minor infractions. It's not clear whether the names of suspended students would be kept confidential or if a school would be tipped off if a student with a record of violence transferred to another school.

Several months after Fralick's death, a student task force presented a report it hopes will help the province reduce bullying at school. The student-led brainstorming sessions were held across Nova Scotia. Students felt teachers and counsellors didn't have the skills to deal with the bullying that was going on. They recommended that Health offices be set up in every junior high and high school in Nova Scotia. The task force said a workshop expressly dealing with bullying should be held every year for teachers and guidance counsellors.

Naniamo, British Columbia

Jenn Newman started picking on other kids when she was in Grade 1. She threw things at her teachers and pushed other students around. When she was only 12, she earned the nickname, *'butchy Jenn.'* At 14 she broke another youth's rib. By age 15 she added a broken nose to her credit. Newman was a tormentor - and proud of it. Newman was once one of about 1,000 elementary students in Nanaimo, British Columbia who were school yard bullies.

Newman said her motivation was low self-esteem. Even though her mother continually told her she was pretty and smart - it wasn't enough. She needed reaffirmation from her peers. *"I was never good in school. It embarrassed me. I tried to compensate by being tough."* She said. *"The only way I would stop pushing other kids around was if they didn't succumb to the playground thug. A bully wants you to stick up for yourself. If they confront you back - you're going to stop."* Her targets were *"anyone who wasn't my friend"* or anyone who *'wasn't cool'."*

Jer Doney was on the other end of the spectrum. Grade 8 was hell for him. He was picked on regularly when he went to school. Doney used to be one of up to 3,000 students in Nanaimo-Ladysmith elementary schools who were bullies' prey. *"Guys used to come up to me and push me around and stuff,"* he said. Being bullied was only one factor that led to Doney's poor attendance record at school.

"I didn't like school. I just couldn't handle it." he said. Doney and Newman were both kicked out of their regular high school for causing problems and for being absent too many times. They now go to Five Acres Alternate, a school with only 36 students. It is specially programmed to deal with and help kids who are bullies or have other problems. But not every child involved in an aggressor/victim situation can deal with their problems by going to a special school. And for parents of children being bullied every day in regular elementary schools, their lives can quickly turn to shambles.

Nanaimo mom Lynn said she couldn't wait until school break last year, so her son would be out of school and the tormenting would stop. When her son started grade 4, another student started calling him names. Then other students joined in. The bullying ranged from pinecone throwing to name-calling. He was tormented and teased so badly by another; he'd just leave school and go home. Daily abuse turned Lynn's son into an enraged boy who couldn't bear going to school. He gave up all forms of sport - wouldn't do his homework and was angry all the time. Home was the only place he could go where he wouldn't get picked on. The continual bullying eventually resulted in Lynn's son pulling a knife on another student who was teasing him. *"If you get picked on every day - eventually you're going to get to a point where you've just had enough,"* Lynn said. *"It started out with one kid, and then it escalated to others."* She and her family were called in for anger management courses to address the boy's problems, but unbeknownst to them, the principal of the school never called the parent of the bully.

"The school was part of the problem. They should have handled it better. They should never have let it go on for a year." Lynn's son is doing better now. The bully's mom eventually found out what was going on and told her son how being picked on and tormented every day could make someone feel. She taught him empathy.

Lynn's son also benefited from a session with a counsellor, who told him he wasn't to blame and there was nothing wrong with him. He advised that kids like Lynn's son should change their body language to avert a bully. They should make eye contact with the bully and stand up straight. They should also get an adult to help deal with the situation.

Students are taught that they shouldn't fight back physically if confronted by a bully, but they should not allow the bully a sense of domination. They must learn to be assertive - not passive and how to make direct eye contact.

MVR of **Nanaimo, B.C.** says, *"My daughter was physically assaulted by bullies, and the bullying continued into junior high. One day when she was running for the school bus, one of her tormentors stuck his toot out - she fell and hurt herself and smashed the radio we'd given her for Christmas. When she was eight two boys her age pinned her arms back and a 14-year-old swung a kick, which hit her in the side of her face, breaking her glasses.*

"Besides the physical assault, there's the emotional bullying. These bullies also threaten any kid who wants to be friends with the victim, which further increases their feelings of isolation. Like many of my generation, we thought our children 'had' to go to school. If I had known then what I know now, I'd have taken my daughter out of school and home schooled her.

"The school system failed her then and seems to still be failing kids. My heart goes out to them, particularly the girl who had to leave school because of bullying. She's right - she shouldn't have to leave. Most bullies have a pattern of this type of behaviour, and after being warned once, if the offence is repeated they should be permanently expelled.

"All too often, the bully's parent is in denial. When I phoned the mother of a notorious bully, she asked plaintively, 'Why does everyone blame my son?' One can barely begin to imagine the despair some of these kids must feel, to conclude that the only solution is to take their own lives. My heart goes out to their parents."

Calgary, Alberta

Matt Haghighi says, *"How can kids have so much hatred in their hearts and minds? Where does all this hatred come from? And finally, how could anyone hate such a beautiful girl like Amanda Philips?*

"Schools should have codes and policies framed in every classroom and in the hallways, with strict adherence to them. Policies such as zero tolerance for bullying, intimidation, harassment, discrimination, making fun of an individual, foul and offensive language, and zero tolerance for the use of the word hate towards an individual. Kids,

guilty of the above should be thrown out of schools, and their parents should be held accountable.

"When will we as parents live up to our responsibilities? Schools should be institutions for academic and social studies not institutions of Hell, distress and grief.

"As to that principal, who wants proof for everything in life - all he needs is a complaint from two individuals. Why do we always have to wait for somebody to die to act? What would happen to schools in Canada if guns would be readily available, like the US?"

Laura Hatch of Calgary states, "As a mother of two teenagers, I am sickened by the blind-eye attitude of (officials at a college in Manitoba). To deny a problem on the word of the 'bully' is truly pathetic. The victim and their parents are the ones whose word should be taken seriously. Would Mr. Weston and Mr. Wallace recognise a problem at Teulon when one of those bullied students comes to school with a weapon to take revenge on those that are bullying him/her?

"I wonder what their comments to the parents of, say, five or ten fatally injured and innocent students would be. A child who 'just can't take it anymore' needs to know they're not alone and help is there for them, whether it is from the school officials or the community at large."

Edmonton, Alberta

L. Lavallie, Edmonton, Alberta states (regarding a television program on bullying), "I could not help but wake my son up to watch the television program together and we cried. You see the worst of it all is the lack of concern that we have encountered when trying to deal with this subject with teachers or school officials. I almost want to sue the school board myself as this has caused our family tremendous pain in the last three years.

"I have watched as a mother, my son who was a straight-A student, balloon up to 170 lbs at age 11 because of all the anger and frustration he has held inside because of the lack of any support system from the school system. We have even changed elementary schools, and I have discussed the issues at length with past and present principals only to be met with condescending disregard that this is part of the growing up process.

"Well then, please explain why there are so many laws implemented in the workplace to protect adults from even verbal abuse and yet I do not know where to go to protect my child? His outlook on life has changed dramatically and I fear for his future regarding his mental well-being as well as his weight problem. We have already had an incident like this happen in Taber, Alberta and yet this matter is still met with such disregard! I am watching a small child turn into an angry youth each day, and I weep for his lost child-hood. I stay in constant contact with the school, but the most they can seem to do, or will do, is have a talk with the children that they know are problematic and are contributing to this. But I ask - where are the parents in all of this? Why are school officials so afraid to approach these people when the bullies themselves are in so much need of help as well? And why is my child to suffer the consequences of another's actions with no real reprimand being installed to stop this re-occurring violence? Even police officers with guns in their belts can charge someone for threats alone. If grown adults are frightened of this behaviour, why then is it acceptable for children to display it and get away with it?

"I wonder what the quality of my son's life could have been in the last three years had someone even once just believed us when we said that this is very serious for the victims and the bullies! My child has paid a dear price already. I can only hope that someone will listen to us soon before it's too late. I see his hope in everything fading each day, meanwhile the bullies and their parents and the school officials all get to go home and sleep at night. My son cries himself to sleep, then he awakens every day and musters up the strength to face another day of the same horrible treatment and all I can do is hope someone hears us, before he just plain gives up. That truly would be a crime because all I did was raise him to be respectful of others and this has been his reward! I have the dual guilt of knowing that he does not trust my words of hope anymore, and the knowledge that I just cannot protect my child! The bullies of today are the future criminals of tomorrow. How can this not be serious and why are the parents and school officials not accountable?"

Mansfield, Ontario

Sharon Kerpan (commenting on the same television program) says, "Our son, too, has been the object of bullying, physical and verbal. He is small for grade 9, wears glasses, and is involved in theatre, not sports. He gets the 'gay,' 'queer,' 'homo' thing as well as body slamming in the halls, having his body squeezed by the locker door courtesy of his next-locker neighbour, who's much larger and somewhat older. There was also an incident on the bus where his head was shoved against the window with such force that his glasses were bent beyond wearing. At that time, we got as far as calling the police and were ready to place charges but could not get one person to verify his story, so we dropped the issue, hoping that the school would act. Very little was done, and the insinuation was that our son must have done something to antagonise this other boy (who has been in trouble before for physically acting out) as if that was justification for violent behaviour.

"Dale has been the victim of taunting, pushing, body checks, etc. almost daily, although lately he says things have improved a little as he tries to turn slights into jokes - 'improv' acting style. Kids don't want to make an issue of behaviour like this because they fear that it will only make things worse - and often it does.

"When our child comes home crying at the age of 14, you know that something is terribly wrong in his school life. When attempts to bring attention to this kind of bullying in a 'zero tolerance' environment, are met with hesitancy, you know that there is something terribly wrong with the existing disciplinary system in our schools, particularly at the secondary level. School administrators seem reluctant to take decisive action in these cases due to public reaction. So many advocacy groups promoting children's rights have left administrators not wanting to cross any lines, real or implied."

Woodstock, New Brunswick

Ann O'Donnell says, "It's a sad day when the adults who are paid well to protect and teach our children are too apathetic or cowardly to do so. The administration of this Manitoba School (in Teulon) has failed not only those students who have suffered at the hands of the 'bullies', but also those children who commit such cowardly acts. I was appalled by the principal's lack of response and even more so by that of his supervisor - neither of those people have 'earned their keep.' I felt sad that they chose the standard response of defending their ineptitude, rather than being proactive. My other question is "Where are the parents of these so-called bullies, and why have they not been active in seeking help for their children?" Bravo to the principal and staff of Seaview School for providing instruction and support to both groups of children. This approach takes high energy and much effort, but our children are worth it!"

Winfield, British Columbia

Gerry M. Laarakker states, *"There's an important aspect being overlooked, that of kids being bullied by their teachers. Who does not remember this from their own experience, or who among us have not seen an element of that in their children's school experience? I know I have, and so have my children."*

Squamish, British Columbia

Frank W. Baumann states, *"I'm amazed that all the experts and their comments focus on laying down the law and punishing bullies, rather than asking why bullying happens in the first place. When children are bombarded every day with hockey violence, television violence, movie violence, video game violence, is it any wonder that they eventually get the message that physical and mental bullying is the way to solve problems and deal with frustrations?"*

Quebec

Tom Connolly of Low states, *"From experience, I have little doubt that bullying is the root cause of most of the mass shootings covered in the news in recent memory. It is not guns, not TV, nor violent video games and music. They, at most, simply provide a means to visualise one form of retribution - one that, unfortunately seems more simple and accessible than our justice system.*

"I believe the long-term solution lies in poking our resources against the broad topic of intolerance, rather than the individual issues - like racism and bullying - that comprise it. For now, more aggressive tactics like surveillance and isolating either the bullies or the victims might be warranted.

"Pre-emptively, school administrators and society in general must begin to respect the seriousness of the bully issue. It literally, can be life threatening to both the tormentors and the 'apex victims' - those at the bottom of the pecking order - alike."

Saskatchewan

A 17-year-old male in Saskatchewan says the abuse can be physical and emotional, such as classmates ridiculing his appearance and calling his mother a prostitute. *"No matter what school I went to, everyone gave me a hard time. From grades four to seven, I have moved to different schools hoping that there would be one where teachers and students were nice - but I never have."*

Taber, Alberta

In April 1999, a 14-year-old boy entered W.R. Myers High School in Taber, Alberta, shot and killed a 17-year-old student, **Jason Lang** and badly wounded his 17-year-old friend **Shane Christmas**. It was Canada's first fatal high school shooting in 20 years. The shooter had been an *'at home'* student. He did his schoolwork at home because he feared school. Shortly after this shooting, the Alberta government amended their School Act that obligated school boards to develop and implement written policies addressing physical violence, sexual assault and threats or intimidation of any kind.

In a series of columns on the tragedy in Taber, CBC News Online learned from classmates that the boy was *'everybody's best punching bag.'*

Bill 206 - The School (Students' Code of Conduct) Amendment Act, 2000 was introduced partially in response to the school shooting and death of Jason Lang. That amendment can be viewed on-line at:

http://ww.qp.gov.ab.ca/Documents/acts/S03.CFM

Ron Henry, a 15-year-old student said, *"He sometimes was body-checked into the lockers. They'd try to pick fights with him and he'd just take it. They knew he wouldn't fight back."*

Surrey, British Columbia

The family of a 14-year-old boy who committed suicide blames his death on constant teasing and bullying at his high school. **Hamed Nastoh** was a Grade 9 student at Enver Creek Secondary School in Surrey. He described the harassment he suffered in a seven-page note he left for his family (who had no idea of Hamed's troubles at school), before leaping to his death from the Patullo Bridge.

Hamad's grieving mother, Nasima Nastoh, says her son told the family in his note that bullying and taunting drove him to suicide. And the letter said, *"Mom, I was teased at school by my mates, my classmates, even my own friends laughed at me. They always called me four-eyes, big-nose, and geek, because his average mark was over 90. He had very good marks and he was very intelligent."*

His fellow students constantly called him *'gay'* and *'faggot'*. He had never told his parents he was being bullied.

Muriel Wilson of the Surrey School Board says she tells students there is a zero-tolerance policy on bullying. *"If they witness bullying, they take an active role in trying to stop it. Let us know so we can deal with it. And if the children are being bullied, let us know so we can deal with it."*

But that did not happen in this case. Hamad's mother says he refused to talk to school officials. His friends also felt powerless to stop the taunting he endured. *"Everyone gets bullied. But this went too far. We stood up for him, but people couldn't get the hint that this went too far, and this pushed him,"* says one Enver Creek student.

His mother says one of the last wishes Hamed expressed in his suicide note was for people to stop harassing each other and to realise that teasing is hurtful.

Delta, British Columbia

John Donnelly and **Joy Dorras** of Delta, British Columbia say, *"Our family had an experience we would like to share. We transferred out of the B.C. public school system into a private Catholic School. We felt that the high moral standards promoted by the school would provide a safe environment for our kids where they would learn to share and respect.*

"We were mistaken. Our son, Jordan (now 12), was bullied for three years by a small group of kids, and particularly by a class ring-leader, who gained power over his peers by putting down weaker students. After our first year there, we started noticing behaviour changes in our child's slouching shoulders, wandering alone, and a lack of self-confidence. We were able to identify the problem children who were intimidating and bullying our son and wrote letters to the school principal. We also wrote to the parish priest.

"To our frustration, they did not contact the parents of the bullying kids, or deal with the problem immediately. Yet on the rare occasion where our son tried to fight back, they made him write an apology letter to the bully. We finally recognised there was no chance to win in this school, and that the best thing we could do was to leave. And this has proven to be true. Given a fresh start in a public school in our neighbourhood, our son has made many friends, and his learning has improved tremendously.

"Our advice to educators, who must deal with this first hand, is to send the bully home immediately for the day. Even with slight infractions, call the parents, and get the parents to leave work and

pick him or her up. They will then have to deal with it, and the problem will be out in the open. Principals seem reluctant to send kids home, yet this immediately exposes the bully.

"Our advice to parents is to get out as soon as you can. If you suspect your child is being bullied, then do not hesitate to leave the school. Expose the bully to the principal and the parents - but then leave. Your child most likely will not be able to overcome a bullying system once it begins to develop. Transfer to another school and communicate with other parents to help your child find good friends."

Vancouver, British Columbia

A ghastly instance of bullying happened in Victoria B.C. on November 14, 1997 when fifteen teenagers, mostly 14 and 15-year-old girls, swarmed, attacked, brutalised and beat 14-year-old **Reena Virk** into unconsciousness. Two of the teens **Kelly Ellard**, 15 and **Warren Glowatski**, 16 followed the battered and weak Reena, inflicted other blows on Reena that included slamming her head against a tree. They broke her arms, beat her more and dragged her into the water under a bridge. Then Kelly held Reena's head under the water with her foot (the impression from a runner sole was left on Reena's scalp) while she and Warren smoked cigarettes. Her body was found eight days later in an ocean inlet. Although hundreds of teens knew of the killing - no one spoke up.

Children, said in an essay on the tragedy, that Virk desperately tried to fit in, but she failed. One stated, *"She was brown in a predominately white society. She was supposedly overweight in a society which values slimness to the point of anorexia, and she was different in a society which values 'sameness and uniformity.'"*

Another stated, *"Reasons for being picked on include being fat, thin, tall, short, hair or skin colour, being quiet, wearing glasses, having big ears, small ears, sticky-out ears, crooked teeth, being from a different culture, having different likes or dislikes, the 'wrong' clothes, unwillingness to use strength to defend him or herself, or any perceived or fabricated 'excuse.' These excuses have one thing in common: They're all irrelevant.*

"Each reason is a deceptive justification for the bully to indulge in a predictable pattern of violent (physical or psychological) behaviour against another child who is smaller, younger, or less strong than the bully. In other words, if a child is picked on because they are allegedly

'fat' then losing weight will make no difference; the bully simply invents another justification."

Outside the courtroom, Ellard allegedly bragged about killing Virk, but under oath, she always maintained her innocence.

Six teen-aged girls were convicted of assault causing bodily harm for the initial beating that left Virk staggering and bloodied.

Warren Glowatski and Kelly Ellard were tried in adult court in separate trials. Glowatski was charged and convicted of second-degree murder and is serving seven years without parole in a juvenile detention centre. On March 31, 2000, the then 17-year-old Ellard was convicted of the second-degree murder of Reena Virk and sentenced to mandatory life in prison with no chance for parole for five years.

After serving only one and one-half years in youth custody, Kelly, then 20, was out on bail under house arrest. Her second-degree murder conviction was overturned in October 2001 and she was granted a new trial by the BC Court of Appeals. The court cited improper cross-examinations conducted by the Crown Prosecutors and allegations that the judge in her trial did not properly instruct the jury before their deliberations. Her first appearance at her new trial was February 26, 2003 where her bail was renewed, and she remained under house arrest.

In 2005, Reena's parents Suman and Manjit Virk forgave Warren Glowatski after a meeting with him where he apologized in a heartfelt and genuine manner and promised to try to make a good life for himself after he completed his sentence. Reena's parents went to his parole hearing and vouched for him.

Ottawa, Ontario

April 2000, only five minutes before students of the faculty of Columbine started their one-year memorial service for the massacre that took place on April 20th, 1999 - a 15-year-old male student of Cairine Wilson High School in Ottawa stabbed four of his classmates and a school worker in the back and head with a kitchen knife. The boy got into a fight with other students outside Cairine Wilson library. The principal talked the student into giving up the knife and he was arrested at the scene. His victims - three male and one female student and a school secretary were injured, and the boy was also injured. None of the injuries were serious - all survived and were released from hospital later that day. The student who planned his rampage to coincide with the anniversary, had self-inflicted cuts on his hands, wrists and arms. He had been counting the days to the anniversary of the Columbine incident.

The Cairine student was constantly teased about his severe acne, his baby-face and his curly hair. He was described as a loner. The quiet and reserved teen was often teased and called a loser.

He was charged with one count of attempted murder, five counts of assault with a weapon, one count of mischief and possession of a dangerous weapon.

Chapter 7

CASE STUDIES

UNITED STATES

Colombine, Colorado

(One of the earliest famous mass school killings)

On April 20th, 1999, after being teased for years, two students at Columbine High School in Littleton, Colorado (***Eric Harris***, 18 and ***Dylan Klebold***, 17) killed thirteen classmates and a teacher, left 23 students injured (ten of them in critical condition), before killing themselves. Initially they placed two duffel bags filled with propane bombs in the school cafeteria. They left the school and waited for the bombs to explode. They did not detonate.

The two gunmen re-entered the school wearing black trench coats, fatigues and ski-masks and laughed and hooted while they stormed the school. Their rampage spanned different areas of the school, starting with the cafeteria and ending in the upstairs library where they killed most of their victims. One female student was chased under a table and shot after the gunman said *'peekaboo'*. It was the worst instance of school violence to date. Besides the murders and injuries, the killers caused over $1 million in damages to Columbine High School.

Classmates said the two students were members of a group that called themselves the *'Trench Coat Mafia'*. The Trench Coat Mafia was a group of outcasts who would wear long black coats every day, who bragged about owning guns, and hated blacks, Hispanics and student athletes. The two boys were fascinated with the Nazis and World War II and enjoyed talking in German wearing swastikas on their clothing.

The shooting started at eleven thirty on the morning of Adolf Hitler's birthday. During that time, students and teachers hid in classrooms, closets, or underneath desks. Most who had not been shot remained there for hours after the shooting until police could take them safely out of the building. When an explosive device was found in the parking lot, the bomb squad had to carefully search the lot, school and surrounding area. With hundreds of book bags scattered all over the school this was a formidable task. The bodies of the victims weren't removed from the school until the next day, for fear that there might be bombs attached to them. Sheriff Stone reported that over thirty explosive devices had been found in the school, in the boy's cars and in the surrounding area. Some were quite sophisticated and included lethal pipe bombs, incendiary bombs - plastic containers filled with gasoline and soap and propane-powered nail bombs with timers. One was accidentally detonated when the bomb squad tried removed it. When Harris' home was searched bomb-making material was found.

In March 2003, Judge Lewis Babcock ruled that the families of five students who were killed at the school won the right to question the parents of the two killers and others. Their lawsuit alleged that the parents of the gun-men knew or should have known about the boys' plans. It's also possible that they will question Jefferson County Sheriff's officers because of an allegation that Harris and Klebold were subject of a police investigation more than a year before the Columbine tragedy that they were building pipe bombs and threatening mass murder. The deposition list was finalized in April 2003.

On January 10, 2003 Dylan Klebold's parents gave up their three-year battle to withhold information on his 8-page autopsy report. Under Colorado law, autopsy reports are considered public records, unless their release would do substantial injury to the public interest. The autopsy reports of the two killers and their victims were sealed in May 1999. Klebold's death was attributed to a gunshot wound in the left side of his head. The parents released their records two days after the Jefferson County Sheriff's office released nearly 10,000 pages of Columbine documents.

Court Action

One student **Mark Taylor** related his experience during the massacre. He had been eating his lunch outside the school when **Eric Harris** started shooting him. He was shot between seven and thirteen times - most going right through him. The doctors were not able to determine the exact number, because there were so many bullet tracks. He pretended he was dead and survived. He believes that Eric Harris was forced to take the antidepressant Luvox (Fluvoxamine) and that he didn't know what he was doing. Eric started taking the prescription in April 1998, and shortly before the shooting, his dose was increased. Mark and others are suing Solvay Pharmaceuticals Inc. (its manufacturer) because they believe the mind-altering drug was the cause of Eric's rampage that made him manic and psychotic.

Ann Blake Tracy, who is the director of the International Coalition for Drug Awarness says *"Luvox caused Harris to go on the Columbine shooting spree and the medical history of children who commit violent acts in school should be made public. Suing Solvay for the injuries Mark Taylor suffered is one of the biggest SSRI (selective serotonin reuptake inhibitors) suits we'll ever see. All you need to do is read the Luvox package insert to see that Eric's actions were due to an adverse reaction to this drug. There is no doubt in my mind that Luvox caused Eric Harris to commit these acts."*

Mark Taylor's attorney, John DeCamp, explained that some other families pulled out of the lawsuit. *"These families were told that if they continued to sue and lost the case, they would be sued in return and they'd lose their homes, cars and everything for the rest of their lives. My client (Mark Taylor) is basically judgment-proof. In other words, Mark doesn't have anything."*

In May 2000 Solvay withdrew Luvox from the United States due to declining sales.

In my own research on fluvoxamine, I learned the following about complications that can occur to those taking such a drug:

Physicians prescribing the drug for extended periods need to periodically evaluate the patient;

It is not to be prescribed to children under 18 years of age (Eric was 18 when he died so must have begun his use of it at the age of 17);

Can cause, agitation, nervousness, anxiety, abnormal thinking, depression, abnormal dreams, depersonalisation, psychotic depression, confusion, apathy, hostility, euphoria, neurosis, hallucinations, manic and paranoid reaction, delusions and suicide attempts.

Mattawa, Washington

On April 10, 2001, 16-year-old ***Cory Baadsgaard*** walked into his English class at Wahluke High School in Mattawa, Washington with his father's big game hunting rifle and took twenty-three students and his teacher, Michele Hanson hostage. Hanson and some of the students held hostage made frequent eye contact with Baadsgaard, and calmly talked to him as he sat leaning against a classroom wall clutching the rifle. Principal Bob Webb and intervention specialist David Garcia entered the room and kneeled next to Baadsgaard. Cory surrendered, and no one was hurt. Later a small number of students related that he'd been suicidal - once threatening to jump off a cliff when he was rock climbing. On the other hand, his parents described Cory as a *'jock'*. He was on the basketball team, played golf and football and was very popular at school.

For nine months, Cory had taken the drug Paxil. Three weeks before the hostage-taking he was taken cold-turkey off Paxil and switched to a high dose of Effexor (an SSRI) to treat situational depression. His parents testified that the morning of the incident he had taken about 300 milligrams of Effexor. His father has no doubt that the medication caused the incident. He described Cory's amnesia, hallucinations, and abnormal dreams as side effects of the medication. After Cory was on medication his parents realised that he was having aggression problems that were out of character.

Cory stated that he felt sick that morning and didn't feel like going to school, so he went to bed. The next thing he remembers, he was in juvenile detention centre.

Cory pleaded guilty to 24 counts of third-degree assault and a gross misdemeanour charge of interference by force or violence He was sentenced to 14 months in jail. While he was in jail he wrote letters of apology to classmates he has known since kindergarten. He's now free but must remain under community supervision for five years and seek treatment for the depression that led to the incident.

Cory Baadsgaard (from Mattawa, Washington) and **Mark Taylor** met in January 2003 to discuss their common goal - to lobby against drug companies that produce SSIRs (selective serotonin reuptake inhibitors). Baadsgaard says he also may sue the drug companies and join Taylor in travelling across the USA speaking out. They've also produced a documentary called, *'The Drugging of Our Children.'* against drugs.

January 23, 2003, Belgian chemicals and drug company, Solvay, dismissed claims made in a lawsuit by a survivor of the 1999 Columbine massacre. A court hearing was scheduled for February 5th with the actual trial starting in March.

In February 2003, Mark Taylor withdrew his claim. No money was paid to Mr. Taylor or his lawyers in exchange for the dismissal, but Sovay donated $10,000 to the American Cancer Society. Mark Taylor was left holding the bag for a disputed legal fee of $116,000. (I can't help but wonder whether Mark Taylor too was intimidated so much by the powerful drug company that he dropped his claim.)

Comments from Users of Paxil, Wellbutrin, Zoloft, Celexa, Antivan (Lorazapam) and Effexor
(http://paxil.bizland.com/guestbook.html)

*"I started **Paxil** last year to deal with severe panic attacks. I gained 40 pounds, had no sex drive (just married) and felt like I was walking through a dream each day. I was unable to feel any emotions. I decided I should try another anti-depressant and my doctor recommended **Wellbutrin**. I stopped taking Paxil. I have been in hell ever since. I can't describe the pain and sickness that I have endured. My doctor told me to stop taking the Wellbutrin. Well it's day 13 since I stopped Paxil and I have the worst electric zaps through my entire body and still have not been able to eat a meal and have diarrhoea every day. The nausea is so bad they make me dry heave. I keep thinking that I'm dying. I cry for three hours straight every day. This is so much worse than the panic attacks and no one seems to understand just how ill I am. I have fever, chills - you name it. I am in so much bodily pain that I can't lie down, stand or sit in one place too long. I keep taking Tylenol to ease the body aches - to no avail. I wish someone could help me. I have never felt this helpless before."*

*"I've been taking **Paxil** for about 3 years. One time I tried to get off it and began getting electric shock-like feelings. It got so bad that I couldn't move my head or even my eyes. I thought that if I slept, it would go away, but it didn't. It got so bad that I started taking **Paxil** again. I'm now up to 60 mg and take **Antivan (Lorazapam)**. I still get the shock-like feeling in the night, when I'm walking and need to turn my head suddenly. I found that at 40mg the electric shock was there all the time, but when the doctor increased my dose it went away."*

*"I was on **Zoloft** and it began to work well, to start... but, like others, I began to get electrical pulsing and blurred vision. My doctor then put me on **Paxil**. It worked at first but after a while it was a lot worse. My doctor took me off all medication and said I needed therapy or counselling. Over this time, I felt as if I'd been losing myself. My mother was on **Celexa**, so I tried it. It worked better than the rest, but I began feeling more suicidal, antisocial and feel confused and lost. I think now that these medicines have taken their toll, I might be bipolar with mild schizophrenia."*

*"I have been on **Paxil** since 1993. If I taper off, I feel as if I am going crazy. My brain feels as if it is floating and it must catch up with my body. I have mood swings, feel as if I am dying; my entire world starts*

to fall. I get scared and mad at the same time. I'm so dizzy, I feel as if I am drunk. My doctor insists that I continue with my medication. I now take **Wellbutrin** to counteract my paxil symptoms. We know God did not intend for us to take pills. He intended us to live life to the fullest, with its ups and downs. I want to feel like I did when I was a kid and not on pills."

"I have been taking 20 mgs a day of **Paxil** for the past year with no problems. Then I had one of the rarest and least-documented side-effects from this terrible drug. I had missed one only one nightly dose and not realizing it until late afternoon, took it at 3:00 p.m. the next day. Within 1-hour, strange things happened to me. At first, it was a strange sensation of having to lean to one side when walking. Within 30 minutes it had become slightly painful, and I lay down for a bit. I was having the beginning of a Dystonic reaction, and nothing would get better for many hours. While I was lying down, my muscles started to tense up - first my jaw clenched, then my hands would become fists without me doing it. I phoned my brother and he said he would be over in an hour. I didn't know I was in any danger. Soon the full force of the reaction hit me. My entire body seized up in an incredibly painful series of contractions. My hands became immobile claws, and my head and neck were frozen to one side.

"I was terrified. My tongue curled up in my mouth, and I feared I might swallow it. I called my brother to take me to the hospital. He arrived and carried me to his car and took me to the hospital. They gave me Benadryl IV and in less than a minute, I felt better. I felt my muscles relax and could speak. Blood and urine tests confirmed that the Paroxetine in my body caused the problem. I tried to go cold turkey and get off **Paxil,** but I am getting zapped everywhere. I guess I just must twitch until I can't twitch any more. Wish me luck - I think I'll need it."

California

On March 5th, 2001, 15-year-old honour-roll ninth-grade student **Charles Andrew Williams** (known as Andy) smiled as he shot dead two fellow students and wounded 11 students and two adults at Santana High School. He had fired more than 30 shots in the school with a .22 calibre long-barrelled revolver that he reloaded 4 times. One of the wounded was a sheriff's deputy assigned to the school. Andy had been saving one bullet for himself but was unable to use it because of law enforcement action. Authorities arrested the boy in the bathroom.

Williams had been talking about his planned shooting for several days, but his comments were not taken seriously. He finalized his plans and decided he would proceed with the rampage three days before it happened. As with many cases, initial reports suggest Williams was the target of bullying and teasing about his big ears and *'scrawny'* size that was not dealt with. He was so skinny that some called him *'Anorexic Andy,' 'freak,' 'dork,'* and *'nerd'*.

The shooting spree at California's Santee High School left students, teachers and parents asking themselves if they ignored signs of the impending attack. It was the worst such incident since the Columbine High School killing in April 1999. Killed were students, 17-year-old **Randy Gordon** and 14-year-old **Bryan Zachor**. When he was arrested, Williams was filled with anger and expressed no remorse.

According to friends and an adult acquaintance, only two days earlier he had talked about going on a shooting spree. They thought he was just joking. *"The whole weekend I was with him, he was joking on and off that he was going to come to school and shoot people,"* student **Josh Stevens** said. *"He had it all planned out, but at the end of the weekend he said he was just joking."* Three students who allegedly knew about the attack beforehand were told to stay off campus by school authorities.

Chris Reynolds, whose son was friends with Andy Williams, said the boy had stayed at his house on Saturday night and talked about his plans. *"I even mentioned Columbine to him. But he said: 'No nothing will happen, I'm just joking.'"* He now regrets not acting to prevent the shooting. *"That's going to be haunting me for a long time. It just hurts, because I could've maybe done something about it,"* said Mr Reynolds.

Andy Williams was held on 28 counts that included two counts of murder with special circumstances and 13 counts of attempted and premeditated murder charges of murder, attempted murder and other charges. At his trial, he was sentenced to life in prison with no possibility of parole for 50 years.

Red flags

Experts say that most, if not all, school shooting incidents are preceded by verbal threats and these should be assessed together with other potential warning signs. **Joanne McDaniel from the Center for the Prevention of School Violence** says there are always red flags that must be looked out for. Not a single indicator, she explains, but a set of them over time. Threatening statements should always be investigated. Ms McDaniel says interest needs to be taken if certain indicators are present:

- Withdrawal, or feelings of isolation and rejection
- If a student is bullied or teased - as appears to be Andrew Williams' case
- If they cannot handle anger
- Similarly lack of interest in school, a difficult family life and access to arms - seven rifles were found in the boy's flat - should be considered. *"There is no guarantee that a shooting can be prevented, but there is an opportunity to intervene and some incidents can be averted,"* says Ms McDaniel.

And thanks to special hotlines and tip-offs there have been examples of this. In 1999 a girl alerted her parents about an alleged plot to carry out a Columbine-style shooting spree at a school in Cleveland. Earlier this year, a California student was discovered to have an arsenal of weapons and accused of planning to carry out a shooting at his college.

Kevin Dwyer from the National Association of School Psychologists says, *"The blame rests squarely on the availability of guns and the misdiagnosis of depression. People don't take these kids seriously. They tell friends they're going to do something. They send a lot of signals."*

San Diego, California

Jason Hoffman, 18 arrived at his school, got out of his car, went into a firing position with a shotgun and opened fire. (The rampage occurred three weeks after the shooting by Andy Williams in Santee - 6 miles north of El Cajon.)

As Jason approached the building he was verbally confronted by the dean of students **Dan Barnes**. Hoffman eluded Barnes and ran toward the school administration office, randomly firing into windows. At least eight shots were fired. Hoffman wounded five people, some from the flying glass when shotgun pellets crashed through the window of the administration building. The school security officer, **Richard Agundwz** brought him down in a gun battle. Jason was shot twice - once in the face and once in the buttock.

Immediately after the shootings, Principal **Georgette Torres** ordered a lockdown of the 2,900 students. For as long as an hour, staff and students stayed behind locked doors until the police were sure that Hoffman acted alone.

One victim, 15-year-old, **Andy Yafuso** was in serious condition with between 40 and 50 wounds from buckshot pellets in the face, arms and upper body. A 15-year-old female student, **Shaunda Hughes** was grazed on her right leg, **Carina Schribellito**, 17, and **Jennifer Strom** were wounded, and **Billy Ditzler**, 16, had an arm wound, **Toby Haltstead**, 15, was hit in the arm, and buttocks and had dozens of pellets in his leg. A female teacher, **Fran Zumwait**, was grazed by bullets and received scratches on her face and legs. Social science teacher, **Pricilla Murphy**, was struck in the arm and leg, was treated in hospital and released. Two weapons were recovered - one a pump-action shotgun and the other a handgun.

Hoffman was described as a loner and was often upset for reasons that were unclear. He didn't try to make friends. Some students weren't surprised that the intimidating Hoffman could be capable of such violence. Dan Barnes escaped by ducking into an office after the teen aimed at him. In written statements Jason made to police, he said he felt Barnes was out to get him and was somehow to blame for his inability to get into the Navy.

Hoffman had been receiving treatment for clinical depression before the shooting. He had seen a psychiatrist who had prescribed two anti-depressant medications - Celexa and Effexor.

There's conflicting information about whether Hoffman meant to kill anyone during his rampage. Hoffman told his probation officer, Ron Anderson that it was never his intention to target anybody and noted that he had loaded the weapon with birdshot. He said he had brought along the .22 hand gun, so he could kill himself if all else failed. Immediately after his arrest, Hoffman told police that he had been planning the shooting for years. Hoffman said he had targeted and intended to kill the dean of their school.

Because Jason was 18, he was charged as an adult and faced 27 years to life when he pleaded guilty to one count of premeditated attempted murder and five counts of assault. His sentencing was scheduled for November 8, 2001.

He had been on a suicide watch, but in October 2001, (before he was sentenced) Jason Hoffman committed suicide in jail. He was found hanging from sheets he had shredded into strips that he'd put through a ventilating screen in his cell. Later the Medical Examiner's Office revealed that he had tried to hang himself in jail numerous times before he succeeded. Most of his attempts involved making a noose out of bed sheets so he could hang himself. This raises questions about the quality of care he received and why the jail did not keep him under a more serious suicide watch.

Two weeks before he hanged himself, Jason had told his probation officer the reason why he had opened fire at his school. It was because he wanted a *'cop'* to shoot him to death. And three days before he killed himself, his mother had written a letter to the court about her son's mental problems with clinical depression and his adverse reaction to his anti-depressant medication.

In May 2001 **Tobey Halstead** who had been injured by Hoffman, filed a $250,000 legal claim against the Grossmont Union High School District for negligence in allowing Jason Hoffman to come on campus with guns.

San Carlos, California

In January 1979 - while under the influence of drugs and alcohol, 16-year-old **Brenda Spencer** killed two people and wounded nine with a .22 calibre rifle from her home across the street from San Diego High School to become USA's first high-profile school shooting. Before she surrendered, the school principal, **Burton Wragg** and custodian, **Mike Suchar** were dead, eight children were wounded (including 9-year-old **Cam Miller** who was shot through the back) and a police officer was shot through the neck.

She pleaded guilty to first-degree murder and assault with a deadly weapon and was sentenced to 25 years to life in prison.

Wisconsin

Jamie Nabozny was harassed, spit on, mock-raped while other students laughed, urinated on, called a *'fag'* by a teacher and kicked repeatedly in the stomach by his fellow students. This happened at Ashland Middle and Ashland High Schools in Wisconsin from the time he was in grade seven until grade eleven. He had stomach aches every day and lived in fear when he got on the school bus. He had to use bathrooms usually used by teachers to avoid students in their own bathroom.

The name-calling started after students found out that Nabozny had been the victim of sexual abuse by his youth minister at his church. He identified that he was gay when he was eleven years old and told his parents who took a while to accept his new status.

Jamie reported his physical and verbal harassment to school officials, told them he was gay and demanded the abuse stop. It would settle down for a while but would always start up again. He stated, "Everybody was afraid to talk to me because other students would think they were gay." His principal did not help. Instead, he made comments such as, *"Boys will be boys,"* and, *"If you're going to be so openly gay, you can expect that kind of behaviour to happen."*

Jamie described himself as a shy, quiet boy who was a good student. He became depressed and tried to end his life three times. At times the only thing that kept him from killing himself was that he didn't want to hurt his mother. He dropped out of school in the eleventh grade.

He sought punitive damages from the school, but he lost the case. The judge who ruled in favour of the school said he believed everything that happened to him, but since he was in a public school, he wasn't protected. Nabozny believes, *"If I was in a mental institution - I would have been protected. If I was a criminal and in jail - I would have been protected. But since school is a voluntary place to be (according to the judge) I wasn't."*

Jonesboro, Arkansas

On March 24 1998, the heavily armed boys hid in the woods behind their school and started firing on students as they exited during a fake fire drill. His grandfather said that Andrew admitted to pulling the fire alarm. The cousins, **Mitchell Johnson**, 13 and **Andrew Golden**, 11, wore camouflage outfits as they fired on classmates and teachers. Ten of the wounded and the five of those who died were all female. Those who died were: **Natalie Brooks, Paige Ann Herring, Stephanie Johnson,** all 12, and **Brittany R. Varner**, *11.* One of the school's English teachers, *Shannon Wright*, 32, was pregnant and might have been an intentional target. She died shielding a child and succumbed to her injuries after surgery to the wounds to her chest and abdomen. Paramedic, Charles Jones told reporters: *"We had children lying everywhere. They had all been shot."*

Mitchell's parents were divorced, and he often ran away from home. Mitchell had recently been dumped by his girlfriend, Candace Porter. He threatened to shoot her, and she was wounded in the barrage. She related that Mitchell often talked about beating up other boys, so she thought little of it when she heard he was saying, *"Something big might happen."*

He had warned his friends that *"He had a lot of killing to do."* He had told friends that he was going to go to school the next day and shoot them. He told his friend Melinda Henson, *"Tomorrow you will find out if you live or die."* Cindy Angel said her step-granddaughter and Stephanie Johnson, one of the girls who was killed, had come home from school the day before the shootings and talked about threats Mitchell Johnson had made. *"He said he was going to kill the girl who had broken up with him and the others who had made him mad and Mrs. Wright. I didn't think much of it."*

Friends and neighbours described eleven-year-old Andrew Golden as evil, demented, a troublemaker who was always threatening people. His father was the registered representative for a local gun club. The day of the massacre the boys stole weapons (rifles and handguns) from Andy's grand-father's shed.

The two boys were held on murder and battery charges while they waited for a court appearance on April 29th. They were charged as juveniles, each with five counts of capital murder and ten counts of first-degree battery. Juvenile court found them guilty, but all Judge Ralph W. Wilson Jr. could do was sentence them to Juvenile Prison, perhaps until they turn 21.

Moses Lake, Washington

In 1996, when **Barry Loukaitis** (an honour student) was 14, he broke into an algebra class at his school dressed like a gunslinger and started shooting with his two concealed pistols, seventy-eight rounds of ammunition and a high-powered rifle. The first student to be hit was 14-year-old **Manuel Vela**. He then shot another classmate in the chest and his teacher in the back as she was writing a problem on the blackboard. His fourth bullet hit a 13-year-old student in the arm. Another student was shot in the abdomen and right arm. Two students and the teacher died.

Loukaitis then took hostages but allowed the wounded to be removed. **Jon Lane**, a physical education teacher at the school and champion wrestler lunged into the room, disarmed Barry and held him until the police arrived.

Loukaitis blamed his act of terror on *'mood swings'*. On his father's side, the family had a history of depression that went back four generations. A psychiatrist said that Barry had delusional, godlike feelings before his deadly rampage and was not able to distinguish right from wrong at the time of the killings. One of his fellow students claimed that Loukaitis had stated that it would be fun to go on a killing spree. The prosecutors alleged that Loukaitis had planned the shootings carefully - that it wasn't a sudden act.

Orin Bolstad, a child psychologist who treats young killers in Oregon's juvenile prisons, testified at his hearing. He spent 36 hours talking to him, gave him a battery of tests and is convinced the 17-year old was psychotic, depressed and suicidal. He also believes that he suffers from paranoid schizo-phrenia or the manic phase of bipolar disease.

He was sentenced to life in prison.

Springfield, Oregon

On May 20 1998, **Kipland Kinkel** was arrested and expelled from school on a charge of possessing a stolen firearm. He was released to his school teacher parents (Bill and Faith Kinkel's) custody. Kip was terrified of his father, felt that he couldn't live up to his popular and athletic older sister, and felt he had nowhere to turn. His choice was to end his parents' lives. Bill was sitting at the kitchen counter drinking coffee when Kip fired one shot in the back of his father's head with his .22 rifle. He dragged his body into the bathroom and covered it with a sheet. His Mom was not at home at the time. He spoke several times to others on the phone while he waited for her to return home. No one knew that he had killed his father.

He met his mother in the garage, told her he loved her, and then shot her twice in the back of the head, three times in the face and one time through the heart. He dragged her body across the garage floor and covered her with a sheet. After he killed his parents he spent the night with their bodies while he booby-trapped his home with bombs.

The next morning, dressed in a cream coloured trench coat he drove his mothers' Ford Explorer to school. He shot **Ben Walker** and **Ryan Atteberry** on the way to the cafeteria and opened fire on students in the cafeteria of Thurston High School. He fired 51 rounds from his .22-caliber Ruger semi-automatic rifle. He also had a .22-caliber Ruger semiautomatic handgun and a 9mm Glock semiautomatic pistol and several fully loaded ammunition clips.

He killed two students, 17-year-old **Mikael Nicholauson** and 16-year-old **Ben Walker** and wounded 22 others. **Jake Ryker**, a 17-year-old wrestling student had been shot in the hand and chest, but tackled Kipland as he was re-loading his gun. Others piled on to pin Kipland until police arrived. He had a knife taped to his leg which he attempted to use against the arresting officer. The officer had to subdue him by spraying him with pepper spray.

In Grade Four, Kip was diagnosed as having a learning disability (dyslexia) but had above-average performance in science and math.

At one literature class at his high school, Kip read from his journal about his plans to *'kill everybody'*. When he was in the seventh grade, his parents discovered that Kip had downloaded bomb-making instructions. In September 30, 1997, he allegedly gave a talk in speech class about how to build a bomb and bragged about torturing animals. Kip had once told Nissa Lund that he'd once stuffed lit firecrackers in a cat's mouth. His former girlfriend said he boasted about shooting little cats and was talking about blowing up a cow.

His mother Faith, at least acted to try to help her son. In January 1997, she took him to a psychologist, Dr. Jeffrey Hicks. The psychologist talked to Kip about *his* guns and *his* satisfaction with *his* Glocks. Not surprisingly, Kip developed an obsession with Glocks. Hicks advised that Kip be placed on Prozac, and in June 1997 Kip began taking 20 milligrams per day. Dr Hicks stated there was a vast improvement in Kip.

In June 1997, his father bought him a 9mm Glock 19 - one of the guns used in the killings to divert his son's obsession with weapons into a supervised hobby. On July 30 1997, Dr. Hicks, Faith and Kip all agreed that Kip was doing well enough that he could discontinue treatment.

Shortly after, Kip bought a .22 pistol from a friend and kept it hidden from his parents. In the fall of 1997, Kip stopped taking Prozac. On September 30, 1997, his father bought the .22-caliber Ruger semiautomatic rifle for his son under the condition that he would use it only under adult supervision. The day before he shot his parents Kip purchased a stolen .32 calibre Beretta semiautomatic pistol for $110 from a school mate, **Korey Ewert**. When the gun was reported stolen, the police were called, and Kip admitted having the gun in his locker at school. Both he and Korey were arrested, handcuffed and suspended from school.

Since early adolescence Kip had been involved in petty theft, and he'd been slowly arming himself with numerous guns, shell casings, a hand grenade and explosives. When the police searched his family home they found detailed bomb-making instructions, various chemicals used in explosives, five sophisticated bombs, and fifteen other inactive explosive devices. One of the bombs was found under his mother's body. As the bomb squad were removing one device, it accidentally detonated.

Kinkel was charged with four counts of aggravated murder and was indicted on 58 felony charges including four counts of aggravated murder. Judge Jack Mattison sentenced him to 111 years in prison, without the possibility of parole. When his attorned asked the Supreme Court to review his case, the Court of Appeals ruling upheld the sentence.

Denver, Colorado

January 2003 - Denver police will likely file reckless endangerment charges against two 10-year-old fifth-grade ringleaders at Harrington Elementary School who were accused of poisoning an eleven-year-old girl's drinks. The girl said that seven of her classmates (five girls and two boys) slipped pills, glue and other items into her water and soft drinks on three occasions. At least one of the students told her she was going to die of poisoning. The girl did not drink the beverages - and did not become sick.

The police are investigating what kind of pills was involved. They believe that the girls brought the medications from home and intentionally put them in the girl's drinks. They explained that they didn't like their victim and they wanted to hurt her. The students involved were not known troublemakers, and their school principal Sally Edwards said, *"I was totally shocked. They are all good students."* The students were suspended for five days. Some could face expulsion.

Maquoketa, Illinois

During the 2000 - 2001 basketball season, **Michael Delaney**, 14 was repeatedly harassed and beaten on bus rides to basketball games, in the locker room at away games and at school. While two coaches were on the bus, sitting right behind the driver, he was assaulted at the back of the bus for about 25 minutes. Four of the team members twisted Michael's nipples so hard that bruises and black marks were left. Michael was hit and choked with the chain from his grandfather's military dog tags. The boys put black tape on Michael's face and told him he couldn't take it off.

In the locker room when he was just wearing his under shorts, Michael was hit on his legs, head, arms and body with a leather belt. At another game, Michael was whipped 12 to 15 times with a leather belt causing bruises and welts. He didn't fight back and at first didn't tell his parents, because he was afraid the situation would only get worse.

Eventually the school learned about the beatings. Four upperclassmen: senior **Keith DeMoss** and juniors **D.J. DeMoss, Evan Sikkema** and **Justin Sommers** were accused of attacking Michael and admitted what they had done so. They were not suspended from school but were not allowed to play with the basketball team for the remainder of the season and not allowed to participate in any other extracurricular activities for six weeks.

After a trial Michael and his parents sued the Andrew Community School District that was ordered to pay $100,000 for not supervising bus rides and locker rooms sufficiently enough to prevent hazing. Michael received $75,000 and his parents $25,000.

Lincoln Park, Michigan

After kissing her reflection goodbye, 12-year-old **Tempest Smith** hung herself from her bunk bed. Her journal outlined her private thoughts about her daily struggle with the incessant teasing she faced daily. She spent much of her time alone in her bedroom writing poems. She was a very pretty, tall slim blond and it's hard to believe that others teased her - but they did because she was so shy, for her choice of wearing dark *'Gothic'* clothing to school and about her religious beliefs associated with witchcraft. Tempest's mother Denessa said that Tempest had told her teachers about the teasing all the time. *"I have to wonder if someone at the school shouldn't have stopped it,"* she said.

Her classmates at Lincoln Park Middle school are now facing the task of finding reasons to account for the torment they put her through. Many explained that they feel responsible because they teased her so ruthlessly.

Only four Michigan children in her age group committed suicide in 1995, but by 1998, 13 had taken their lives. Officials believe that teasing pushed these already troubled children over the edge.

Chapter 8

CASE STUDIES JAPAN AND GERMANY

JAPAN

The parents of a 15-year-old junior high school girl who committed suicide in October 2000 by hanging herself, filed a 44-million-yen damage suit against her school because it failed to address the bullying that was behind their daughter's death. Their daughter was allegedly the target of persistent schoolyard bullying by students at Yushu Junior High School in Ichihara, Chiba Prefecture. Her parents had repeatedly called the school to ask them to stop the bullying.

Their daughter was discovered dangling from a tree with a rope tied around her neck. Police discovered a note in the girl's bedroom waste basket that said, *"I will never forgive them. I will get my revenge on them."*

The school admitted that they were aware that she had been bullied by four or five boys. The boys told her she stank and wrote messages on her desk demanding that she kill herself. The school held class meetings and moved the bullies away from the girl and they thought the bullying had stopped. They said the girl didn't look depressed. On the day she hung herself and was absent from school, the boys (unaware that she was dead) put a flower on her desk and prayed as if they were having a funeral for her.

GERMANY

Erfurt, Germany

Expelled student, **Robert Steinhaeuser**, 19 entered the Johann Gutenberg High School walked the halls hunting down 13 teachers, a 15-year-old male student and a 14-year-old female student. He gunned down a female police officer who was the first to respond. Six others were wounded with the 9 mm Glock handgun and pump-action shotgun he carried.

The siege ended when **Rainer Heise**, a history teacher, pushed Robert into a classroom, tore off his mask and locked the door. Robert killed himself just before police reached his location.

Wozinkel, Germany

In 2001, while his parents were out shopping, **Christian** poured petrol over himself and set fire to it before hanging himself from a staircase at the family home in Wozinkel, Germany. He left a note that read: *"To my friends, parents and others, this will be my last letter because I am going to hang myself. My life is shit. I have hardly any friends, bad marks at school. But I am doing it mainly because the big right-wing radicals at my school beat me up all the time."*

Their son was still burning when they arrived home. After the tragedy, his friends confirmed that four boys with skinhead haircuts and combat boots often teased, pushed and beat him.

Meissen, Germany

In November 1999, after taking bets from his classmates that he would dare to commit the crime, a 15-year-old boy stabbed his 44-year-old teacher to death. The betting pot had reached $500. He was rewarded by seven years in jail.

North Rhine-Westphalia

A couple in Germany have been forced to pay compensation for attacking members of a female gang who bullied their son at school. The couple went to the school in Altenbeken, in North Rhine-Westphalia, and ended up pulling the gang members' hair.

Paderborn County Courts ordered them to pay around £1,500 pounds for their unacceptable behaviour and a further £305 to the research fund at Altenbeken High School. The father told Bild newspaper: *"It was worth it - since then our son hasn't received any hassle."*

Head teacher, **Hermann Knaup**, said *"This type of incident was unusual at the school"* which he said experienced *"the usual types of fights- no different to anywhere else."*

Chapter 9

HOW TO PREVENT AND STOP SCHOOL BULLYING

Every child has the right to an education and has the right to be safe. Adults working the school systems have a duty to provide a safe school environment for all students. Safe schools are:
- Free from violence
- Nurturing, caring and respectful of everyone;
- Physically and psychologically healthy;
- Advocates of sensible risk taking;
- Enhance the self-esteem of all.

What parents can do when a child complains of being bullied

When a parent finds out his or her child has been bullied, the initial feelings are of outrage and anger and their first reaction is to act and take steps to stop the bullying. But what are they to do?

If the child is physically injured, these would need to be attended to first. If possibly take coloured photos of the injuries and/or any damage there may be to the child's clothing or belongings. Sympathize with the child and let him/her know that this is a case of bullying and you will be taking steps to stop it from happening again. Interview any witnesses. If injury is serious, lodge an assault case with the police against the bully. If the child is afraid to have you say anything, explain that if s/he does nothing, it protects the bully who is counting on the child not to *'tattle'*.

Write down all the details about the incident - what happened, where it happened, who was involved and names of any witnesses. If the bullying took place on school property, speak with the school principal and give a copy of your written notes about the bullying incident. Add the school's reactions to your complaint, giving name of person, staff position, date and time of interview. Schools have a legal responsibility to ensure that they will provide a non-violent environment for all students.

Contact the parents of the bully. Many will co-operate, but others don't see the bullying actions as being important enough to deal with it. In the latter homes, violence and abuse are usually the normal behaviour so the parents will not be concerned about doing something to stop the bullying. Point out that there was physical damage (either to the child or his/her possessions) and that what has happened is assault. Explain that you will be reporting it to the school and it could become necessary to contact the police. Let them know you're serious about your complaint. Let them know what you expect them to do:

Have the bully apologize to your child.

Determine what punishment the child will have for the bullying incident and what they will do if the incident happens again.

Warn the child that if this behaviour happens again, that you will go to the police and charge them with assault.

Parents of a bullying child need to ask themselves whether their actions to each other in the home have contributed to their child believing that bullying is acceptable behaviour.

If the school or parents do not show that they will deal with and stop the bullying, go higher in the school system. If this doesn't prove successful, send a copy of the report of all events to date to the police for their files and advise them that you are seeing a lawyer. If you can't afford a lawyer, low cost legal aid is available in most cities.

When a child is enrolled in a school, the parents should ask for copies of school policies relating to bullying and what steps they should take should an incident take place. They should insist that they be informed of all bullying incidents that occur that affect their child (whether as a victim or as a witness).

Anti-Bullying Policies

Many schools have an unofficial reputation for tolerating bullying. This reputation is usually common knowledge throughout the student community. In these schools more children tend to feel anxious about their personal safety and as a result many are reluctant to attend.

To tackle bullying you will have to liaise closely with the school and will probably have to talk to the bully's parents. Establish first whether this is an isolated incident (in which case nipping it in the bud is likely to have a high probability of success) or whether the child bully has a history of bullying behaviour. Remember that most children will try bullying at some time. Most will soon realize that it's not an appropriate way of behaving and grow out of it quickly, especially if you help your child see why it's inappropriate and encourage and support them in learning better ways of behaving.

Only when the issue of bullying is brought into the open and policies and procedures showing how the school will deal with bullying are widely known *and enforced* will schools gain a reputation for being safe for *all* children. Even students who can't be categorized as victims or bullies, but who might witness bullying, feel more comfortable when they know that the school stands against bullying. When children know that the school they attend has a *'zero tolerance'* to bullying and have an Anti-Bullying plan in force, they can then concentrate on their studies.

When they enter a school with a Zero-Tolerance for bullying, students who have bullied before usually test the policy. Transferring student records should be examined to see if there were any bullying incidents at their last school. The Zero Tolerance school must instruct new students about the school's bullying policies and procedures. School faculty must maintain a high profile in terms of the behavioural expectations of their students to gain support and trust from the students. A commitment by the staff to no-bullying in the school must be a long-term undertaking.

Schools can crate support groups where victims can concentrate on developing coping skills needed to change their place within the social hierarchy. The goal is for the victim to become a part of the group of students who do not bully and are not bullied. Such changes require a great deal of time and effort, but it's possible, given the necessary support of parents, schools and the community at large.

Students are the key to a successful Anti-Bullying campaign primarily because they usually know who the bullies are long before the adults do. They are more likely to support an Anti-Bullying campaign if they are directly involved in determining the need for such a program and its implementation. This includes developing anti-Bullying policies and subsequent school-wide activities with instructions on what should be done if bullying is witnessed. School authorities need to make students feel secure that teachers ensure that the information they share will not cause them to lose status in their peer group. Confidentiality must be maintained so the program must be seen by the students as workable. Students need to understand the differences between ratting and reporting incidents.

'Ratting' occurs when a student tells about an inappropriate act with the idea of getting another student into trouble.

'Reporting' happens when a student tells to protect the safety of another student.

Once students understand the difference between the two, reporting bullying incidents becomes much less of a social taboo.

Each school should have a clearly written school behaviour policy that includes school bullying and hazing. There should be clear boundaries between what is acceptable and what is not. It should be linked to a system or rewards for good behaviour and should promote respect of others and intolerance of bullying behaviour. Those who do not follow the policy should receive counselling on how to raise their self-confidence level in other ways than bullying others. Bullies will be shown how they can be more self-disciplined and empathetic and know what the consequences will be should their behaviour not fit the school behaviour policy. They must know that there is a zero tolerance to bullying at the school.

Chapter 10

HOW TO PREVENT AND STOP SCHOOL BULLYING

AUSTRALIA AND NEW ZEALAND

Australia's Commonwealth Government, in a national inquiry into school violence (Sticks & Stones, 1994), concluded that bullying was a significant problem in Australian schools. The inquiry called for the development, implementation and evaluation of intervention programs to reduce bullying. Partly as a response to this call, an intervention called P.E.A.C.E. Pack:

A program for reducing bullying in our schools was developed. The acronym P.E.A.C.E. represents the various stages in the process for initiating, conducting and evaluating a program for reducing school bullying (Preparation, Education, Action, Coping and Evaluation). The program, now in its third edition has been widely used in Australia and in several other countries and translated and evaluated in countries such as Japan.

Australia has a multitude of excellent anti-school bullying programs available. The question is - why is school bullying increasing and becoming far more violent - rather than decreasing? If these programs were effectively implemented, there would be far less bullying in our schools. Only a coordinated effort of our government, the departments of education, the schools themselves, the police, the entire community and parents will we stamp out school bullying! I believe that the Federal Government Department of Education should put in place anti-bullying policies and procedures that should be used in *every* school in Australia. This way, consistency would be kept, and all children would be protected. That policy should include professional counselling for both the bully and the bullied, until their behaviour is stabilised.

Our children are constantly exposed to violence - and I don't just mean watching gun battles and murder scenes on the television. Have you really paid attention to what they're watching in our sports-addicted society? If you have, you'll notice how much aggression and violence is now used in the name of *'sport'*. Grown men poke other players, gouge bodies, and generally act the part of the school bully. And we wonder why our children clone that behaviour! Our society needs to look seriously at cleaning up the violence we now see in several of our sports. Sport used to be *'sportsmanlike'* but the violent actions we see in our football players – can't be called sporting at all.

When you consider that fifty-six per cent of Victorians aged 11 to 21 (surveyed by the Sunday Herald Sun) reported being victims of schoolyard bullying - and 69 per cent in the 11 to15 age group these programs need the help of the entire community to change bullying.

Queensland Teachers Union President, Ian Mackie said that teachers had reported an increase in racial vilification in the school yard. Michele Elliott, the author of Bullying is a British publication, but it is relevant to Australian children.

They can relate to comments made by children like 13-year-old Katherine who talks of the pain of being given the silent treatment: *"They called it 'being sent to Coventry'. Since no one would talk to me, I couldn't even find out why they were being so horrible. I had done nothing to them. It wasn't fair."*

Elliott notes that girls are becoming more physical in their bullying techniques. 14-year-old Lisa states, *"My friend Susie was beaten up by a gang of girls. She had her nose broken and ended up in hospital ... I couldn't believe that girls could act like that."*

Elliott's advice includes what to do if you are being bullied by a teacher and how to make friends, but, most of all her message is, *"Don't accept that you have to be a victim."*

Marten wore glasses, and when he was eleven, he felt desperate. His father helped him come up with smart replies: *"It felt stupid saying them out loud at home and I didn't think they would work. The first time I tried one of them out, the bully was so surprised that he backed off. Everyone else laughed with me - not at me."*

Victoria's worst behaved schoolchildren are being asked to sign good behaviour contracts in last-ditch bids to avoid expulsion. Department of Education and Training show 188 primary and secondary school students were expelled between February and August of 2001.

Some of the students are as young as nine. Swearing, disruptive behaviour in class, bullying and missing lessons are some of the reasons behind the thousands of contracts are signed each year. The contracts, are signed between parents, the school and the child, but *not* legally binding. (I think they should be because these students are wasting the taxpayer's money by wasting their portion of the school taxes). They are used when other disciplinary methods such as report cards and detention fail.

The contracts apply to situations that have become serious - where discussions and negotiations with the child and/or parent haven't gone anywhere.

They include the behaviour expected of the student and the consequences should they not comply. Parents or guardians are often signatories. Students who break contracts generally face suspension or expulsion. These contracts don't work without the full support of students, teachers and parents. *"The contracts aren't worth the paper they're written on unless you've got commitment from all parties,"* said Victorian Association of secondary School Principals deputy president **Andrew Blair**.

"A significant number of students take contracts as their wake-up call," said Education Services Minister **Monica Gould**. She added that the Government had introduced several programs to improve behaviour, with a major focus on stamping out bullying. The Government had also spent more than $50 million annually to employ school nurses, student support service officers and student welfare co-ordinates.

Guidelines on Countering Bullying Behaviour in Primary and Post-Primary Schools –September 1993 - Victorian Association of State Secondary Principals

Introduction and Background

Since 1990 the Minister for Education has issued several Circular Letters to the Managerial Authorities and Principal Teachers of Primary and Post-Primary Schools on:

a. Guidelines Towards a Positive Policy for School Behaviour and Discipline,
b. A suggested Code of Behaviour and Discipline, and
c. Procedures for Dealing with Allegations or Suspicions of Child Abuse.

Those Circulars comprehended the issue of bullying within the general context of School Behaviour, Discipline and Child Abuse. The positive role played by school management, teachers and parents in countering bullying behaviour is acknowledged. However, the incidence and nature of bullying is such that the Minister now considers that additional measures are required to deal specifically with the problem.

The aims of the **'Guidelines on Bullying'** presented here are twofold, firstly to assist schools in devising school-based measures to prevent and deal with bullying behaviour and, secondly, to increase the awareness of bullying behaviour in the school community as a whole e.g.: school management, teaching and non-teaching staff, pupils and parents/guardians as well as those from the local community who interface with the school. It is of importance that the issue of bullying behaviour be placed in a general community context to ensure the co-operation of all local agencies in dealing appropriately with it.

The role of the school is to provide the highest possible standard of education for all its pupils. A stable, secure learning environment is an essential requirement to achieve this goal. Bullying behaviour, by its very nature, undermines and dilutes the quality of education and imposes psychological damage. As such, it is an issue that must be positively and firmly addressed through a range of school-based measures and strategies through which all members of the school community are enabled to act effectively in dealing with this behaviour.

Bullying behaviour affects not only those immediately involved; it affects everyone in the classroom, in the school community and, ultimately, in the wider community. It is recognized internationally that bullying behaviour is not confined to pupils and schools alone; it is prevalent in society, in the workplace and in the home.

Bullying behaviour thrives in an atmosphere of uncertainty and secrecy in which the victim often feels a sense of hopelessness and futility against the power being exercised by the bully; a high degree of collective vigilance is needed throughout the local community, the school, and other agencies and by parents if bullying behaviour is to be identified and dealt with in a fair and equitable manner.

Definition of Bullying

Bullying is repeated aggression, verbal, psychological or physical conducted by an individual or group against others.

Isolated incidents of aggressive behaviour, which should not be condoned, can scarcely be described as bullying. However, when the behaviour is systematic and ongoing it is bullying.

[**Note:** Ask an adult who was bullied as a child and they will tell you that one incident was serious enough that it traumatized them for a life.]

Types of Bullying

Pupil Behaviour

Physical Aggression: This behaviour is more common among boys than girls. It includes pushing, shoving, punching, kicking, poking and tripping people up. It may also take the form of severe physical assault. While boys commonly engage in *'mess fights'*, they can often be used as a disguise for physical harassment or inflicting pain.

Damage to Property: Personal property can be the focus of attention for the bully: this may result in damage to clothing, school books and other learning material or interference with a pupil's locker or bicycle. The contents of school bags and pencil cases may be scattered on the floor. Items of personal property may be defaced, broken, stolen or hidden.

Extortion: Demands for money may be made, often accompanied by threats (sometimes carried out) in the event of the victim not promptly *'paying up'*. Victims' lunches, lunch vouchers or lunch money may be taken. Victims may also be forced into theft of property for delivery to the bully. Sometimes, this tactic is used with the sole purpose of incriminating the victim.

Intimidation: Some bullying behaviour takes the form of intimidation; it is based on the use of very aggressive body language with the voice being used as a weapon. Particularly upsetting to victims can be the so-called *'look'* - a facial expression that conveys aggression and/or dislike.

Abusive Telephone Calls: The abusive anonymous telephone call is a form of verbal intimidation or bullying. The anonymous phone call is very prevalent where teachers are the victims of bullying.

Isolation: This form of bullying behaviour seems to be more prevalent among girls. A certain person is deliberately isolated, excluded or ignored by some or the entire class group. This practice is usually initiated by the person engaged in bullying behaviour. It may be accompanied by writing insulting remarks about the victim on blackboards or in public places, by passing around notes about or drawings of the victim or by whispering insults about them loud enough to be hears.

Name Calling: Persistent name-calling directed at the same individual(s), which hurts, insults or humiliates, should be regarded as a form of bullying behaviour. Most name-calling of this type refers to physical appearance, e.g. *'big ears'*, size or clothes worn.

Accent or distinctive voice characteristics may attract negative attention. Academic ability can also provoke name-calling. This tends to operate at two extremes; first, there are those who are singled out for attention because they are perceived to be slow, or weak, academically. These pupils are often referred to as *'dummies,' 'dopes'* or *'donkeys.'* At the other extreme are those who, because they are perceived as high achievers, are labelled *'swots', 'brain-boxes', 'licks', 'teachers' pets'*, etc.

Teasing: This behaviour usually refers to the good-natured banter that goes on as part of the normal social interchange between people. However, when this teasing extends to very personal remarks aimed again and again at the one individual about appearance, clothing, personal hygiene or involves references of an uncomplimentary nature to members of one's family, particularly if couched in sexual innuendo, then it assumes the form of bullying. It may take the form of suggestive remarks about a pupil's sexual orientation.

Bullying of School Personnel

Bullying of school personnel by means of physical assault, damage to property, verbal abuse, threats to people's families etc.

Teacher Behaviour:

- A teacher may, unwittingly or otherwise, engage in, instigate or reinforce bullying behaviour in several ways:
- Using sarcasm or other insulting or demanding form of language when addressing pupils;
- Making negative comments about a pupil's appearance or background;
- Humiliating directly or indirectly, a pupil who is particularly academically weak or out-standing, or vulnerable in other ways;
- Using any gesture or expression of a threatening or intimidatory nature, or any form of degrading physical contact or exercise.

Effects of Bullying

Pupils who are being bullied may develop feelings of insecurity and extreme anxiety and thus may become more vulnerable. Self-confidence may be damaged with a consequent lowering of their self-esteem. While they may not talk about what is happening to them, their suffering is indicated through changes in mood and behaviour. Bullying may occasionally result in suicide. It is, therefore, important to watch for changes in behaviour as early intervention is desirable.

Indications of Bullying Behaviour – Signs and Symptoms

- The following signs/symptoms may suggest that a pupil is being bullied:
- Anxiety about travelling to and from school,
- Requesting parents to drive or collect them,
- Changing route of travel,
- Avoiding regular times for travelling to and from school,
- Unwillingness to go to school,
- Refusal to attend,
- Deterioration in educational performance,
- Loss of concentration,
- Loss of enthusiasm and interest in school,
- Pattern of physical illnesses (e.g. headaches, stomach aches),
- Unexplained changes either in mood or behaviour, (it may be particularly noticeable before returning to school after weekends or more specifically after longer school holidays),
- Visible signs of anxiety or distress – stammering, withdrawing, nightmares, difficulty in sleeping, crying, not eating, vomiting, bedwetting,
- Spontaneous out-of-character comments about either pupils or teachers,
- Possessions missing or damaged,
- Increased requests for money or stealing money,
- Unexplained bruising or cuts or damaged clothing,
- Reluctance and/or refusal to say what is troubling him/her.

Those signs do not necessarily mean that a pupil is being bullied. If repeated or occurring in combination, those signs do warrant investigation to establish what is affecting the pupil.

Characteristics in Bullying Behaviour

Schools need to recognise that any pupil can be a victim of, or perpetrator of bullying behaviour.

The Victim:

Any pupil, through no fault of his/her own, may be bullied. It is common during normal play for pupils to tease or taut each other. However, at a certain point, teasing and taunting may become forms of bullying behaviour. As pupils are particularly quick to notice differences in others, pupils who are perceived as different are those more prone to encounter such behaviour. However, the pupils who are most at risk of becoming victims are those who react in a vulnerable and distressed manner. The seriousness and duration of the bullying behaviour is directly related to the pupil's continuing response to the verbal, physical or psychological aggression.

It is of note that some pupils can unwittingly behave in a very provocative manner that attracts bullying behaviour.

The Bully

It is generally accepted that bullying is a learned behaviour. Pupils who bully tend to display aggressive attitudes combined with a low level of self-discipline. They can lack any sense of remorse; often they convince themselves that the victim deserves the treatment meted out.

Pupils who bully can also be attention-seeking; often they set out to impress bystanders and enjoy the reaction their behaviour provokes. They tend to lack the ability to empathise. They are unaware or indifferent to the victim's feelings. Others seem to enjoy inflicting pain. It is of note that many bullies suffer from a lack of confidence and have low self-esteem. It is not uncommon to find that pupils who engage in bullying behaviour are also bullied. They tend to be easily provoked and frequently provoke others.

Where does Bullying Happen?

(a) Pupil Behaviour

Bullying in schools frequently takes place in the playground. School playgrounds with hidden or obscured parts may provide an environment conducive to bullying. Many of the games which pupils play present possibilities for bullying because of their physical nature. It is relatively easy to single out and harass another pupil. The noise level masks much of what is going on. The playground provides the opportunity for older pupils to pick on younger pupils. The playground is also the ideal setting for the *'bully gang'*. Continuing provocation may eventually lead to a physical fight, and ironically in some cases the victim may appear to be the aggressor because s/he finally gives vent to his/her frustration. Toilets, cloakrooms, locker areas, changing rooms and showers may be the scene of verbal, psychological and physical harassment. The behaviour of pupils in these areas needs careful monitoring.

Bullying may also take place in class. It may occur subtly through glances, looks and sniggers but may take the more overt form of physical intimidation. It may also be exacerbated if a classroom atmosphere prevails whereby pupils can make derogatory comments about their classmates or other teachers. However, teachers need to be alert to the underlying reasons for such comments in case pupils are trying to disclose something that is disturbing them and thus needs further investigation.

Bullying may also occur between classes irrespective of whether the class or the teacher moves. In the former situation the bullying goes on in the corridors and corners, while in the latter case the classroom is the arena for various forms of hurtful behaviour.

The area immediately outside the school, the local shops and local neighbourhood are often the scenes of bullying. Bullying also takes place on the journey to and from school, whether the individuals are walking, on bicycles or on school busses.

(b) Teacher Behaviour

The teacher behaviour of a bullying nature is referred to in Section 3 (b) is most likely to take place in a classroom situation, but not exclusively so. Such behaviour may, for example, also take place in the school playground, gymnasium or the sports field.

Prevention of Bullying

The Circular Letters issued by the Minister for Education to the Managerial Authorities and Principal Teachers of primary and post-primary schools referred to in the Introduction comprehended the issue of bullying behaviour in schools within the general contest of School Behaviour, Discipline and Child Abuse. The prevention of bullying should be an integral part of a written Code of Behaviour and Discipline in all primary and post-primary schools. These Circular Letters stated, inter alia, that *"Codes of Behaviour in schools should be considered in the context of the school being a community of which mutual respect, co-operation and natural justice are integral features."*

International research clearly indicates the crucial importance of the existence of a School Policy, which includes specific measures to deal with bullying behaviour within the framework of an overall school Code of Behaviour and Discipline. It is considered that such a code, properly devised and implemented, can be the most influential measure in countering bullying behaviour in schools.

While it is recognized that home factors play a substantial role in the prevention of bullying, the role of the school in preventive work is crucial and should not be underestimated. School-based initiatives will either reinforce positive efforts or help counteract unsuccessful attempts of parents or guardians to control unacceptable behaviour.

Managerial authorities of primary and post-primary schools recognized by the Minister for Education are responsible for the management, organization and administration of the schools and are, therefore, responsible for ensuring the adequate and reasonable measures approved by them to counter bullying are in operation in their schools. The managerial authority of each school in developing its policy to counter bullying behaviour must formulate the policy in co-operation with the school staff, both teaching and non-teaching under the leadership of the Principal, and in consultation with parents and pupils. In this way, the exercise of agreeing what is meant by bullying and the resultant development of school-based strategies for dealing with it, are shared by all concerned. It is essential that all parties concerned have a clear understanding of the policy aims and content if the policy is to form the basis for developing effective school-based strategies for dealing with the problem.

The policy must be promoted by the school Managerial Authorities within the school to all pupils, parents, and staff on a repeated basis with attention being given to incoming pupils and their parents.

Elements of Policy:

Policy Aims:

- To create a school ethos which encourages children to disclose and discuss incidents of bullying behaviour.
- To raise awareness of bullying as a form of unacceptable behaviour with school management, teachers, pupils, parents / guardians.
- To ensure comprehensive supervision and monitoring measures through which all areas of school activity are kept under observation.

- To develop procedures for noting and reporting incidents of bullying behaviour.
- To develop procedures for investigating and dealing with incidents of bullying behaviour.
- To develop a programme of support for those affected by bullying behaviour and for those involved in bullying behaviour.
- To work with and through the various local agencies in countering all forms of bullying and anti-social behaviour.
- To evaluate the effectiveness of school policy on anti-bullying behaviour.

An active school policy on Bullying is most effective when integrated in a school climate, which encourages respect, trust, caring, consideration and support for others. As pupils model their behaviour on the behaviour of adults, Principals and teachers must be careful to act as good role models and not misuse their authority. Moreover, they should be firm, clear and consistent in their disciplinary measures. Techniques based on positive motivation and recognition have been shown to be more effective in promoting desired behaviour than methods that are based on threat and fear.

As self-esteem is the single most influential factor in determining behaviour and indeed a greater predictor of success than intelligence, teachers should provide pupils with opportunities to develop a positive sense of worth.

Research has shown that pupils can achieve significantly more in classroom situations where they are rewarded for effort and improvement and where expectations of their performance are positive. An integral part of this approach is the development of co-operative learning. A pastoral care system should operate in schools whereby designated teachers would seek to build up a relationship of trust and confidence with their pupils with a view to preventing cases of bullying behaviour.

Note: Factors having their origins in difference of conflicts between parties outside the school, may contribute to increased incidents of bullying within the school.

Drawing up a School Policy for Dealing with Bullying Behaviour

Elements of School Policy

School Ethos

At the centre of a whole-school response to bullying is the creation of a positive school climate that focuses on respect for the individual. The prevalent misconception among adults and many pupils that bullying is a normal phase of development that teaches pupils to toughen up, needs to be challenged. It is important that pupils are encouraged to report incidents of bullying. This may require a change in attitudes so that pupils realize that they have a responsibility for the safety and welfare of fellow pupils.

The school behaviour policy should underwrite the non-bullying school ethos. The school Board of Management must approve and endorse this policy. The Principal has a key role in dealing with bullying behaviour in school because s/he is in a strong position to influence attitudes to and set standards in dealing with such behaviour in school. If staff, pupils and parents/guardians are involved in the development of the policy, they are more likely to actively support it. The policy should stress the need to prevent and not just control bullying. It is not sufficient to discipline the bully and to give support to the victim. Following an incident of bullying the issues relating to the prevention of bullying need to be examined. Aspects may need to be altered which may make bullying less likely in the future. It is desirable that there be a consensus within the school community on how bullying in the school should be treated and the creation of a proper school atmosphere is, therefore, beneficial towards this objective. Raising the awareness of bullying as a form of unacceptable behaviour with school management, teachers, pupils and parents / guardians is paramount.

Each school must raise the awareness of bullying in its school community so that they are more alert to it and its harmful effects. Schools may choose to have a staff day about bullying complemented by an awareness day for pupils and parents/guardians. This may help the development and adoption of an anti-bullying code. Such a code will give the parents / guardians of a pupil who is a victim the confidence to approach the school and will also send a clear message to the parents/guardians of a pupil who is engaged in bullying behaviour that they have a major responsibility in changing their child's behaviour. The anti-bullying code should be included as part of the School Plan/Policy Statement and should be available to all by way of a written Code of Behaviour and Discipline for the school.

It is of note that teachers can influence attitudes to bullying behaviour in a positive manner through a range of circular initiatives. In English, there is a wide range of literature available that could be used to stimulate discussion. In Social Studies the inter-dependence of people in communities at local, national and international levels is stressed. In Geography and History references to colonization and exploitation and the long line of dictators could be used to illustrate the negative aspect of power. The work could be extended into Art, Drama, Religious Education, Physical Education etc. Co-operation and group enterprise can be promoted through team sports, clubs and societies in schools as well as through practical subjects. Sporting activities can provide excellent opportunities for channelling and learning how to control aggression.

[**Note:** Schools must deal quickly and effectively with any bullying or unsportsmanlike behaviour displayed during sporting activities, whether it is from the players, the coaches or from their audience. Often their parents can display very aggressive behaviour and encourage the same in their children].

Programmes such as the Stay Safe Programme in primary schools, Health Promotion in schools and various other social, health and media education programmes can further help to address the problem of bullying behaviour. In addition, schools might organize an awareness day on discipline in general and on countering bullying behaviour.

Published material on bullying from various sources mentions the use of anonymous questionnaires to ascertain pupils' perceptions of bullying behaviour. Schools should be aware of the possible abuses that can arise from use of such questionnaires and should exercise extreme caution should they choose to use them. If used, questionnaires should not be used to identify the pupils involved, but only to ascertain the extent and type of bullying, where it happens and the level of reporting, etc.

Comprehensive supervision and monitoring measures through which all areas of school activity are kept under observation. It is important and, indeed, it is the responsibility of the school authority in conjunction with staff and pupils to develop a system under which proper supervisory and monitoring measures are in place to deal with incidents of bullying behaviour. Such measures might include control of school activities on a rota basis. Senior pupils can be a resource to assist in countering bullying. School councils, where applicable, and other school clubs and societies may also be of assistance. It would, of course, be most desirable that non-teaching staff be part of the process in measures to counter bullying behaviour in schools. Also, schemes need to be developed to involve all parents/guardians.

Procedures for Noting and Reporting an incident of Bullying Behaviour

School authorities should ensure that there is a procedure for the formal noting and reporting an incident of bullying behaviour and that such a procedure should be seen to be an integral part of the Code of Behaviour and Discipline in the school. This system should, also, provide for early detection of signs of indiscipline and/or significant change in mood or behaviour of pupils.

All reports of bullying, no matter how trivial, should be noted, investigated and dealt with by teachers. In that way pupils will gain confidence in *'telling'*. This confidence factor is of vital importance. Serious cases of bullying behaviour by pupils should be referred immediately to the Principal or Vice-Principal.

Parents or guardians of victims and bullies should be informed by the Principal or Vice-Principal earlier rather than later of incidents so that they are given the opportunity of discussing the matter. They are then able to help and support their children before a crisis occurs.

Parents or guardians must be informed of the appropriate person to whom they can make their enquiries regarding incidents of bullying behaviour that they might suspect or that have come to their attention through their children or other parents/guardians.

It should be made clear to all pupils that when they report incidents of bullying that they are not telling tales but are behaving responsibly. Individual teachers in consultation with the appropriate staff member should record and take appropriate measure regarding reports of bullying behaviour in accordance with the school's policy and Code of Behaviour and Discipline.

Non-teaching staff such as secretaries, caretakers, cleaners should be encouraged to report any incidents of bullying behaviour witnessed by them, or mentioned to them, to the appropriate teaching member of staff.

In the case of a complaint regarding a staff member, this should normally in the first instance be raised with the staff member in question and if necessary, with the Principal.

Where cases, relating to either a pupil or a teacher unresolved at school level, the matter should be referred to the School's Board of Management. If not solved at the Board level, refer to local Inspectorate.

Procedures for Investigating and Dealing with Bullying

Teachers are best advised to take a calm, unemotional problem-solving approach when dealing with incidents of bullying behaviour reported by pupils, staff or parents / guardians. Such incidents are best investigated outside the classroom situation to avoid the public humiliation of the victim or the pupil engaged in bullying involved, to get both sides of the story. All interviews should be conducted with sensitivity and with due regard to the rights of all pupils concerned. Pupils who are not directly involved can also provide very useful information in this way.

When analysing incidents of bullying behaviour, seek answers to questions of what, where, when, who, and why. This should be done in a calm manner, setting an example in dealing effectively with a conflict in a non-aggressive manner.

If a gang is involved, each member should be interviewed individually and then the gang should be met as a group. Each member should be asked for his/her account of what happened to ensure that everyone is clear about what everyone else has said.

If it is concluded that a pupil has been engaged in bullying behaviour, it should be made clear to him/her how s/he is in breach of the Code of Behaviour and Discipline and try to get him/her to see the situation from the victim's point of view.

Each member of the gang should be helped to handle the possible pressures that often face them from the other members after interview by the teacher.

Teachers who are investigating cases of bullying behaviour should keep a written record of their discussions with those involved. It may also be appropriate or helpful to ask those involved to write down their account of the incident.

In cases where it has been determined that bullying behaviour has occurred; meet with the parents or guardians of the two parties involved as appropriate. Explain the actions being taken and the reasons for them, referring them to the school policy. Discuss ways in which they can reinforce or support the actions taken by the school.

Arrange follow-up meetings with the two parties involved separately with a view to possibly bringing them together later if the victim is ready and agreeable. This can have a therapeutic effect.

Program for work with victims, bullies and their peers

Pupils involved in bullying behaviour need assistance on an ongoing basis. For those low in self-esteem, opportunities should be developed to increase feelings of self-worth. Pupils who engage in bullying behaviour may need counselling to help them learn other ways of meeting their needs without violating the rights of others. Victims may need counselling and opportunities to participate in activities designed to raise their self-esteem and to develop their friendship and social skills whenever this is needed.

Research indicates that pupils identified as low achievers academically tend to be more frequently involved in bullying behaviour. It is, therefore, important that the learning strategies applied within the school allow for the enhancement of the pupil's self-worth. Pupils who observe incidents of bullying behaviour should be encouraged to discuss them with teachers.

School working with and through the various local agencies in countering all forms of bullying as an anti-social behaviour

As previously stated, there should be a whole-community approach to the problem of bullying behaviour. The school as a community is made up of management, teachers, non-teaching staff, pupils and parents/guardians. However, incidents of bullying behaviour extend beyond the school. It is known that they can occur on the journey to and from school. It is necessary, therefore, for anti-bullying school policy to embrace, as appropriate, those members of the wider school community who come directly in daily contact with school pupils. For example, school bus drivers, school traffic wardens and local shopkeepers could be encouraged to lay a positive role in assisting schools to counter bullying behaviour by reporting such behaviour to parents and/or schools as appropriate. Through such approaches, a network is formed.

In certain cases, however, it may be necessary to invite the assistance of other local persons and formal agencies such as general medical practitioners, health boards and their social workers and community workers.

A positive community attitude and involvement can, therefore, assist considerably in countering bullying behaviour in schools. The promotion of relevant home/school/community links is important for all schools regarding countering bullying behaviour and should be encouraged as a normal part of the school's effective operation.

Evaluation of effectiveness of school policy on bullying behaviour

As part of the evaluation of the effectiveness of school policy on preventing and dealing with bullying, a programme of support for those pupils involved in bullying behaviour should be an integral part of the school's intervention process. It is advisable to monitor the effectiveness of school policy on this issue. Random surveys could be held to ascertain the level and type of bullying behaviour in school.

A school's anti-bullying code should be subject to continuous review in the light of incidents of bullying behaviour encountered. It could be included as an item on the agenda for school staff meetings.

Considerations in outlining a positive school policy on countering bullying:

The School:

- Acknowledges the right of each member of the school community to enjoy school in a secure environment.
- Promotes positive habits of self-respect, self-discipline and responsibility among all its members.
- Disapproves of vulgar, offensive, sexist or other aggressive behaviour by any of its members.
- Has a clear commitment to promoting equity in general and gender equity in all aspects of its functioning.
- Has the capacity to change in response to pupil's needs.
- Identifies aspects of curriculum through which positive and lasting influences can be exerted towards forming pupil's attitudes and values.
- Takes care of *'at risk'* pupils and uses its monitoring system to provide early intervention when/if necessary and responds to the needs, fears or anxieties of individual members in a sensitive manner.
- Recognises the need to co-operate with and keep parents informed on procedures to improve relationships within the school community.
- Recognises the right of parents to share in the task of equipping the pupil with a range of life-skills.

- Recognises the role of other community agencies in preventing and dealing with bullying.
- Promotes habits of mutual respect, courtesy and an awareness of the interdependence of people in group and community.
- Acknowledges the uniqueness of each individual and his/her worth as a human being.
- Promotes qualities of social responsibility, tolerance and understanding among all its members both in school and out of school.
- Share a collegiate responsibility, under the direction of the principal teacher, to act in preventing bullying/aggressive behaviour by any member of the school.

Conclusion

It is evident that bullying is a matter of increasing concern in our schools. It poses very real difficulties, therefore, for school behaviour and discipline. Because of this, it is essential that primary and post-primary schools adopt a policy aimed at countering the problem. This school policy should be drawn up after consultation with all the interests involved, i.e., teaching and non-teaching staff, pupils and parents/guardians.

It is necessary that the school policy should have general acceptance by the partners in the education of the pupils. In that way, it can be effective both from the point-of-view of preventing as well as dealing with bullying behaviour. An understanding of the factors that give rise to bullying is needed as well as sympathetic treatment of all those involved in the bullying behaviour. Furthermore, having regard to the nature of the problem, it must, in certain circumstances, receive the attention of others directly outside of the school community.

In conclusion, the inclusion of a module on bullying behaviour in the pre-service training f teachers would be a positive step in alerting potential teachers to the problems caused by such behaviour in schools. Also, it is considered that the expansion of in-service courses to teachers on aspects of bullying behaviour would be of considerable benefit to the teaching profession in the process of raising awareness and developing techniques to deal with such behaviour.

Ken Rigby's Bullying Pages

Ken Rigby, from the University of South Australia has a wonderful web page: http://www.education.unisa.edu.au/bullying. He specialises in school bullying.

Dealing with School Bullying

The purpose of his web site is to provide information that will help people understand more about bullying in schools and how it can be stopped. It is of special interest to educators, children and parents. Topics covered in his web page are:

- Do interventions to reduce bullying in schools really work?
- Countering bullying in schools;
- Book: New Perspectives on bullying;
- Book: Stop the Bullying!
- Book: Bullying in Schools and what to do about it;
- Defining bullying: a new look at an old concept;
- An introduction to bullying;
- A guide to bullying in schools on the internet;
- Finding out about bullying in your school:
- Questionnaires;
- Does bullying really do children any harm?
- Ken Rigby's research publications on bullying in schools (1990-2002);
- Practical resources for schools.

VicHealth - 'Together We Do Better' Campaign

VicHealth has launched an anti-bullying campaign promoting mental health and factors (i.e.: bullying) that impact on our mental health. Their campaign involves the Centre for Adolescent Health, The Centre for Restorative Justice in Canberra (http://www.aic.gov.au/rjustice), and Kids Help Line (1800 551 800) who took part of their campaign.

"Bullying behaviour in our schools is a long-term mental health issue. If you consider that research shows that up to 30% of depression in young people might be prevented if we could stop bullying." said **Dr Rob Moodie**, CEO of VicHealth.

"School is a microcosm of the greater community, and the group is committed to highlighting what is and what can be done to address bullying behaviour in our schools. The research highlights that schools with a supportive and inclusive school community, where students feel they belong and are appreciated, are less lightly to have high levels of bullying behaviour. Having a positive school environment that the entire school community has helped build, will help prevent bullying from happening in the first place.

"What can we do to address bullying behaviour? What is needed is a community response; just s schools in Victoria have adopted a whole

of school approach to create positive and healthy environments for learning. Bullying is not simply an individual problem, or something that is simply art of the 'Aussie, Aussie, Aussie' way of life.

"Failing to address bullying behaviour sends the message that it is an acceptable behaviour within our schools, homes, sports fields, workplaces and community. It misses the opportunity to build positive, respectful and supportive relationships. If we are serious about addressing bullying behaviour it is important to work together as a community to ensure that bullying is not tolerated in schools or the community."

VicHealth launched the **Together We Do Better** campaign to demonstrate its commitment to mental health and to increase community under-standing of the importance of obtaining and maintaining mental health.

The campaign was also about working to reinforce the idea that *together we do better* as individuals and as a community. Being healthy is about being well physically, mentally, emotionally and socially. And this involves families, schools, workplaces, sports, arts and the community.

Having strong social networks and connections; supportive relationships; freedom from discrimination; feeling safe and secure; having people around you can trust are linked to well-being and good mental health.

The question - do we ever get over it? - is the theme of VicHealth's latest *'Together We Do Better'* ad to highlight the long-term mental health implications of bullying behaviour in the community.

If you consider the health implications of bullying - that victimization and bullying behaviour are related to depression, anxiety, loneliness and low self-esteem - sitting back and doing nothing is not a *'healthy'* option.

If we are serious about addressing depression within our community, we'll have to be serious about tackling bullying behaviour to get to the root of the problems such as depression.

Victorian attitudes identified bullying behaviour as a problem within our community in schools, the workplace, government, media and sporting circles.

91 per cent of those surveyed had been a victim of one or more bullying behaviours. 95 per cent said bullying was never acceptable.

We know that if kids are bullied, have no one to confide in and no one who knows them well, they are more likely to develop risk behaviours.

Our schools can be places where students and teachers work together - places where teachers are supported and respected. Schools are a microcosm of the greater community and VicHealth is working to try and reduce the health impacts of bullying in schools, the workplace and the community. ***Together We Can Do Better!***

Restorative Justice
(www.aic.gov.au/crc/reports/strong/school.html)

Restorative Justice in the school setting began in 1994 when conferencing was first used in the Maroochydore area of southern Queensland. This was followed by a series of trials in 75 Queensland schools in 1995-96, where one person at each school underwent training in restorative techniques for dealing with disputes and conflict. As a result, 89 conferences were held in this pilot study dealing with a variety of incidents in the school environment, including assaults, property offences, truancy and drug offences, as well as bullying and harassment.

Despite the favourable reception, the pilot received, it did not gain financial support of the Queensland Department of Education. Although some schools continue to use the program, its resource-intensiveness and need for cultural change in dealing with behavioural management has meant that the program has been limited in its effectiveness.

However, lessons learned in Queensland have been put to good use in New South Wales, where conferencing was introduced in 1997 into some government schools as part of the NSW Department of Education's *Alternative to Suspension Project*. A pilot of twenty conferences was run - about half of them for incidents of bullying. The Department assessed the program as the most successful technique so far tried in dealing with bullying (internal Departmental report) It has since been used in situations of conflict involving both students, staff and other members of the school community and a trial is underway involving the training so far of 150 school staff State-wide. A major outcome measure for the program is the number of days lost to suspension and exclusion, and to date the numbers have decreased markedly in the trial districts (**David Moore**, Transformative Justice Australia, personal communication). The training program has now been refined so that, instead of single individuals from schools attending the training, schools have most of their staff attend a one-day course on how to apply restorative justice principles in dealing more constructively with school incidents of conflict. The conferences are usually run by school counsellors who already have skills in this area, but the success of the program appears to depend on staff in general putting principles of restorative justice into practice in their day-to-day behavioural management of students and of workplace disputes.

In addition, Lewisham Primary School in Sydney has been the subject of a special behavioural management program under the auspices of the Department of Education. Every teacher in the school has been given twenty hours of training in restorative justice principles and techniques, followed by periodic *'booster'* sessions, which has led to a change in behaviour management culture. This culture change seems to be a vital pre-requisite for restorative techniques to take root in the school setting, and failure to achieve it as was the case in Queensland (Thorsborne & Cameron, 2001) makes program success unlikely to be achieved.

In the Australian Capital Territory, there has been considerable interest in restorative alternatives for behaviour management in schools. In 2000, the ACT Department of Education supported a training session by independent consultants on restorative principles and practices attended by twenty staff from eight schools. The Department recognises bullying and harassment as major problems, but also encourages the use of restorative conferencing in dealing with other conflicts, including conflict between staff in the workplace. An evaluation of the program in the primary, secondary and college sectors of ACT schooling is being undertaken by the Centre for Restorative Justice at the Australian National University.

Process for Dealing with Issues Related to Bullying,

Maroochydore State High School (Queensland)

[Maroochydore State High School has an award-winning anti-bullying school policy:]

Anti-Bullying Policy

Maroochydore State High School has a behaviour management plan that includes strategies for dealing with bullying in schools. Our staff are currently using the Education Queensland Bullying Kit for training of all staff, review of their procedures and consideration of the latest in research and strategies to deal with bullying.

Procedure:

We use procedures for Safety, Respect and Learning in conjunction with the Good Standing Policy for all learners. Maroochydore State High School has been using the following strategies since 1990:

- Using Safety, Respect and Learning;
- Using the five P's (Pleasant, Productive,
- Punctual, Prepared, Positive);
- Using the four C's (care courtesy, cooperation and common sense);
- Modelling by the Principal and Deputies weekly on parades, long with teachers and students' rights and responsibilities;
- Modelling by staff in their classrooms and in the playground;

Modelling through our *'Bully Busters Week'* program - activities; highlighting anti-bullying themes. This includes Bullying Surveys. The Year 8-12 leadership program, allows students to model the desired qualities for their peers.

Our behaviour management plan was developed through and by our school community in 1990 through the impact program. This involved teachers, aides, parents, students and consultants. The plan is under continuous review, (staff meetings, working groups) and training is conducted regularly for incoming staff. 2002 has seen a major review of the Behaviour Management Plan which will take effect from 2003. An induction program is in operation and includes the 10 micro-skills of Behaviour Management.

Maroochydore State High School uses the *'No Blame Approach'* and the Anti-Bullying courses to actively deter students from being bullies, and for victims to become more assertive in their response. Workshops for students in peer mentoring and peer mediation have produced successful outcomes in student care and behaviour.

All students receive a copy of the School's Policy for Bullying and Harassment - *'We Want a Safe School.'*

Process for dealing with issues relating to bullying

What happens when a student has been bullied?

- Students wishing to report an incident can either be referred to a harassment officer or the Year coordinator.
- Harassment officers can only give the student a range of options - they cannot advise the student.

- Options may include making a written statement to Year coordinator, no action at present, parent contact.
- If bullying occurs in the classroom, teachers are requested to record the incident in their teacher referral books and forward it to the appropriate Year Coordinator.

What happens when a report has been made? LEVEL 1

- Victim counselled by Year Coordinator.
- Key bully/bullies identified and interviewed.
- Bully writes a statement in response to victim allegations.
- No blame approach for the bully-parent contact may occur at this stage.
- Bully is on first level of anti-bullying program.

What happens if a second offence occurs? LEVEL 2

- If the bully comes back a second time - five lunchtime detentions doing bully busters program.
- Police liaison officer interviews bully as part of the program.
- Parents contacted and notified of the consequences of the next level.
- Bully on second level of anti-bullying program.

What happens if a third offence occurs? LEVEL 3

- For a third offence, students are recommended for an external suspension.
- Parents contacted and notified of the consequences of next level.
- Recommended to see GO's on return.
- Interview with police on return.

What happens if a fourth offence occurs? LEVEL 4

- Students are externally suspended with a recommendation for exclusion.
- Parents conducted - review of process.
- It is important to note that both victims and perpetrators are counselled regarding employing strategies that may assist them in breaking out of the *'cycle'*.

Centre for Adolescent Health Gatehouse Project Survey

"We know that bullying hurts and is a serious health concern. Our research tells us that young people who are victimised are three times more likely to be at risk of having depressive symptoms when compared to those not reporting such experiences," said Prof George Patton, Director of Adolescent Health, Centre for Adolescent Health.

The Centre for Adolescent Health aims to make the difference to young people's health by advancing adolescent health knowledge, practice and policy. The Gatehouse Project was a research project designed to promote emotional wellbeing of young people in schools, by making changes in the social and learning environments of the school as well as promoting change at the individual level. You can learn more about this project on: http://www.gatehouseproject.com

Victoria Department of Education and Training Student Code of Conduct

This Code of Conduct was formulated and put into place in December 1994. Excerpts from the 34-page document include the following:

Responsibility of school councils and principals

Each school council is responsible for the development of a charter. Each school identifies a specific code of conduct within its school charter. This is subject to review in line with Directorate of School Education accountability requirements. The code of conduct is how school councils are to provide a framework for the management of student behaviour and the enhancement of positive relations in the school.

Through the development of a code of conduct, school councils are to identify goals and standards for student behaviour. The principal will have responsibility for its implementation and enforcement. The council is responsible for monitoring the implementation of the code of conduct, evaluating its success, and reporting to the school community and to the Minister of Education.

The code is to be developed through a process of school community consultation conducted by the school council. Students, parents and staff are to be fully informed of the code and expected to support its implementation. A copy of the code including the Student Discipline Procedures, 1994, should be made available to parents. The code of conduct is a school's public statement on the management of student behaviour. The success of the code of conduct depends on the commitment of students, parents and teachers. This can best be achieved by all the groups working together to reach agreement.

The code of conduct should be a succinct statement presented in a form which can be readily understood by parents, students, school personnel and the local community. It is to be a key component of the school charter.

Each teacher will be responsible for developing classroom strategies consistent with the school's code of conduct. This will include the elimination of all forms of bullying, harassment and violence which obstruct the educational progress of students and the general management of the school. The consequences for breaches of these rules should be well established and consistently applied in the classroom and throughout the school. Consequences should be graded in severity, with emphasis on students being accountable and learning to take responsibility for their behaviour.

To learn more, go to:

www.eduweb.vic.gov.au/bullying/conduct.htm

The Alannah and Madeline Foundation

Buddy Bears Schools' Program

The Alannah and Madeline Foundation was formed in 1997 in memory of Alannah and Madeline Mikac who lost their lives at Port Arthur with 33 others. It is a charitable organisation that raises money to help children who are victims of violent crime and sudden family loss.

Buddy Bear is the mascot of **The Alannah and Madeline Foundation's** (AMF) schools program. AMF has extended this schools program, introducing Little Buddy and the Buddy Bear to children in schools across Australia.

The Better Buddies Program is an extension of the Buddy Bear Program introduced to Victorian schools in 2000. This new program was launched in the last week of February 2003, during **Buddy Bear Week**. The program's strong, positive preventive anti-bullying message - *'You can't be a bully if you're a buddy'* - builds on the great work schools already do every year. The Better Buddies Program provides a positive focus to bring together every school's welfare and discipline policies, buddy program, drug education and anti-bullying programs. The Foundation invites schools *to 'Become a Buddy School by Building Better Buddies'* by supporting and augmenting these programs and policies that are already in place. The Better Buddy Schools Program aims to teach children to care about others around them.

Over 700 schools have already taken part in The Better Buddies Program, enabling it to be developed to have the best value to schools. The Education Resource kit *'Buddy Bear-Buddies Help Out'* is written by the Foundation's Education Projects Director, **Maree Stanley**, a teacher with over 20 years' experience in primary schools. Since joining the Foundation Maree has also extended the program into kindergartens and secondary schools.

Many schools have worked with Maree to *'Become a Better Buddies School.'* Maree is eager to point out that the program is simple and easy to implement in any school. She believes the success of the program comes from the fact that schools adapt the program to suit their school environment. It is important to her that the program is *'taken over'* by students and teachers as they know the culture of their schools and know where it would be best placed, therefore having more impact.

St Joseph's Primary and Curtin Primary School in the ACT have instilled the program into their school policies. Curtin Primary has developed a whole-term focus for the beginning of each school year from Prep to Year 6, called *'Everyone's a Winner'* with the Buddy Bear Schools Program as the focus through each level, while St Joseph's Primary has woven the program into their Behaviour Management and Pastoral Care. Many schools have embedded the Better Buddies Program into their wellbeing charter as Apsendale Gardens Primary, Victoria have. In fact, Buddy Bear is on the Prep Booklist and the school have buddies from Prep to Grade 6, linking the program with their school values.

Purpose

The Foundation developed the character of Buddy Bear and The Better Buddies Program to change the culture in the Australian school system-to make it cool for kids to look after each other. The effects of reducing bullying in the community are now becoming more understood happier kids, faster learning. Children who suffer bullying are sometimes marginalised in their school community and may suffer learning disorders. Bullying may lead to long-term health implications.

"Bullying behaviour in our schools is a long-term mental health issue, if you consider that research shows that up to 30% of depression in young people might be prevented if we could stop bullying." Dr Rob Moodie, CEO of VicHealth Promotion Foundation.

The Education resources are free to schools that join the program. Schools may purchase their own Starter Pack and develop their own Better Buddies Program for their school. Research has shown that the buddy system is one of the key components to creating caring school communities. Monies are raised to help the kids by each school selling Buddy Bears to their school community or using the resources within their own classrooms.

The Buddy Bear Story Book has been certified as *'Best Practice'* by the Department of Education and Training (DE&T) on their website to address bullying behaviour at:

www.eduweb.vic.gov.au/bullying/index.htm

The Better Buddies Program is active in schools across Australia, including Victoria, Tasmania, NSW, ACT Western Australia, South Australia and Queensland. Schools across Australia are welcome to register. Maree Stanley and the team are more than happy to work on the Project with you. Register via the website at:

www.buddybear.com or via email at: maree.stanley@amf.org.au

"For the past two years, the Alannah and Madeline Foundation through its Buddy bear schools Program has been working to prevent violence against children," said John Bertrand AM, America's Cup Hero and the Chairman of The Alannah and Madeline Foundation.

Through programs such as the Better Buddies Program, The Alannah and Madeline Foundation are committed to *'taking care of the little things.'*

The Foundation is committed to working with schools and the community to raise the levels of awareness of bullying as unacceptable behaviour through their positive prevention programs.

Bullying behaviour is not an acceptable part of growing up.

Bullying, like discrimination, racism, harassment, violence, physical abuse and assault are all unacceptable behaviours within our community.

Children have a right to grow up in a safe, non-violent environment.

The Better Buddies Schools Program includes a resource package of educational materials, stories, and other activities to assist schools in developing buddy programs across the school curriculum - includes stories, such as **Naughty Stories for Good Boys and Girls**, by well-known children's author Chris Milen.

The program provides schools with a means to support children - teaching children to appreciate diversity, resolve differences, and to eliminate bullying and other forms of anti-social behaviour - and to celebrate the good work of buddies by undertaking a *'Be My Buddy Day'*. These days involve the whole school community - students, teachers and parents.

The program promotes schools' anti-bullying policies, buddy and peer support programs, transition programs, drug education programs and pastoral care programs. The program aims to:

- Assist children to support their peers;
- Encourage children to love and care for other children;
- Promote a children's understanding that violence is not the solution;
- Promote the concepts of hope and peace;
- Develop children's social skills to enable them to get along with others.

The **Better Buddies Schools Program** has reached more than 270,000 children and families in the past year.

Strategies for Schools

(Recommended by the above organizations)

- Schools can acknowledge that bullying happens and take a public stance on its unacceptability.
- Develop school policies and programs that are aimed at both ***preventing*** bullying and ***dealing with*** bullying behaviour when it does occur.
- Involve the whole school community – students, teachers and parents in resolving problems such as bullying.
- Provide clearly understood processes and opportunities for reporting incidents and concerns.
- Provide for the needs of both the students who are bullied and those who engage in bullying.

- Include non-punitive methods to deal with bullying behaviour.

Strategies for parents and carers

- Watch for the signs that might indicate that your child is being bullied or is bullying others.
- Listen and be persistent in trying to find solutions.
- Avoid labelling or having others label young people as *'victims'* or *'bullies'*. It is important to concentrate on behaviour rather than on an individual or individuals.
- Be aware of your own emotions - parents can often experience a range of emotions, including anger, anxiety, sadness, shame.
- Expect support from the school and seek to work cooperatively to find solutions.
- Be familiar with school policy and try to work within it. If dissatisfied with the outcomes, seek further meetings with year level coordinators, student welfare staff or other appropriate staff.
- Work with your child to develop strategies for dealing assertively with bullying behaviour – you may need help from others including school staff, your GP, a counsellor.

Strategies for students

- Remember that lots of people have been bullied at some time in their lives - if it happens to you, you are not the only one and it's not your fault.
- Tell someone - parents, carers, friends, or a trusted teacher. Bulling is against school rules.
- People who mistreat others keep their power when people say nothing. Avoid being a silent bystander when others are being bullied.
- Get help to work out a plan of action - the solution may not be simple, but there are lots of things you and others can do to improve the situation.
- Call Kids Help Line 1800 551 800 if there is no one else you can talk to.

Institute of Criminology study

Shame, rather than blame is the best way to stop schoolyard bullies an Australian Institute of Criminology study has found. The study recommends bullies are made to attend *'victim conferences'* in the same way that criminals are sometimes ordered by the courts to face their victims.

The study's author, Dr Brenda Morrison, said traditional methods of punishing young bullies had been proven not to work. Instead, punishment set up a vicious cycle in which the bully stayed angry and did not confront the shame of their behaviour. *"It sets up what has been called a shame-rage cycle where they continue to lash out at themselves and at others,"* Dr Morrison said. *"The shame is still in them, but they're not really dealing with it. Schools using exclusionary (punishment) models are basically dumping the problem on wider society because research has shown bullies are much more likely to abuse drugs and alcohol and commit crime in later life."*

Dr Morrison said, *"Both the bully and the victim had to learn how to manage their shame. The bully had to be encouraged to take responsibility for (his/her) behaviour by facing the victim and apologizing. In turn, victims would feel better about themselves if they were given the opportunity to accept the apology."*

The study based on two Year Five classes over two terms, found students' feelings of safety at school increased significantly after participating in the project. The model uses role-playing methods to help the children examine their feelings and behaviour in different situations. Before the activities, more than a quarter of the students admitted to using shame displacement strategies (avoiding responsibility) by blaming others for their behaviour or acting out their frustration in other ways. Only 13 per cent reported using these strategies after the project. At the beginning of the study, one-third of students said they would feel rejected by others if they did something wrong, while only one-fifth said they felt that way at the end.

Bullying No Way! Campaign

Philosophy: Australian school communities working together to build safe, supportive, respectful and inclusive environments for every member of the school community - empowering students to be active in the pursuit of justice.

The ***Bullying No way!*** Project is developed and managed by all participating Australian education authorities; State and territory government education systems, the National Catholic Education Commission, the National Council of Independent Schools' Associations and the Commonwealth Department of education, Science and training.

The project has been initiated and supported by Australia's Conference of Education Systems Chief Executive Officers (CESCEO) and the

Ministerial Council on Education, Employment, Training and Youth Affairs (MCEETYA) Student Learning and Support Services Taskforce through the project Safe and supportive school environments: Finding workable solutions for countering bullying, harassment and violence in schools.

Funding for the project comes from the State and Territory government education systems and the Commonwealth Department of Education, Science and Training. The work of the project is supported by teachers, parents, students, staff and curriculum officers throughout Australia. Project materials have been published by Education Queensland for Australian Education Authorities. Harassment based on sex, race and disability is unlawful under the Commonwealth Sex Discrimination Act 1984, and the Queensland Anti-discrimination Act 1991.

Education Queensland currently manages the web site on behalf of all participating Australian Education Authorities.

(This material is reproduced from Bullying. No Way: www.bullyingnoway.com.au The Bullying. No Way! Website is a product of the collaboration of Commonwealth, State, Territory, Catholic and Independent education authorities. The material is reproduced with permission of the Department of Education and the arts, PO Box 10533 City East QLD 4002 Australia, which administers the website on behalf of these Australian education authorities. Educational institutions are granted a free, non-exclusive licence to reproduce, communicate and store this material for educational purposes, but are not permitted to alter or amend the material without the written permission of the Department of Education and the Arts.

Aims of the *Bullying. No way!* Website

- To provide a nationwide resource of State and Territory approaches to minimising bullying, harassment and violence in schools.
- To develop a framework for sharing
- Australian school community solutions that work.
- To use technology and networks to make this information as accessible as possible to school communities.
- To make sure that all students can learn in a safe and supportive school environment.

Bullying. No way! is grounded in national and international documents.

The website furthers the goals identified by the *Adelaide Declaration on National Goals for Schooling in the Twenty-first Century* (1999) by assisting school communities in the development of safe, supportive and nurturing environments where:

Schooling contributes to the development of students' sense of self-worth, enthusiasm for learning and optimism for the future and Students can exercise their rights and responsibilities as citizens of Australia.

The website supports the *United Nations Convention on the Rights of the Child* (UNCRC) treaty by encouraging school community environments that allow children to grow up in an atmosphere of happiness, love and understanding.

How the site can be used

Bullying. No way! includes lots of information that could be used in many ways.

- Teachers and carers could use the site as a basis for developing strategies to assist preschool and primary school children to gain awareness and knowledge, develop positive attitudes about themselves and act for change.
- Secondary students could find the site a useful starting point for discussion, assignments and action planning so that they are active participants in shaping their community.
- Carers could use the site to develop useful ways of communicating with the school to resolve specific issues and to actively participate in school planning processes to build safer and more supportive environments.
- Primary and secondary school teachers could use the site as a curriculum resource and discussion starter for a wide range of issues across the curriculum.
- Whole school communities - students, carers, staff, agencies and community groups could use the site to access:
- A common language to identify misuses of power, clarify the issues and address bullying behaviours;
- Stories and resources that promote understanding and responsive action;
- Information useful for developing and reviewing whole school approaches to safer, more supportive school environments.

- Tertiary students and media professionals can access resources and case studies of effective practice that could complement theory and research.

The Behaviours

"You can't start to think about 'bullying' without thinking about 'power' or in particular 'inter-personal power' or 'relationships power'." **Deputy principal**

Bullying, harassment, violence and discrimination are harmful behaviours that deprive individuals and groups of their rights, jeopardise physical and emotional safety and undermine the wellbeing of our school communities and society.

The role of power: Imbalance and misuse of power underpin every instance of bullying, harassment, discrimination and violence.

Types of behaviour: Open and agreed understanding of bullying, harassment, discrimination and violent behaviour is the beginning of any comprehensive strategy to prevent these problems in schools and increase the wellbeing of our communities.

Implications: Bullying, harassment, violence and discrimination are harmful to both victims and perpetrators.

Communities speak: Voices from school communities express their views on the role of power and the implications of harmful behaviours.

Deeper issues: School communities can be positive spaces where students learn about who they are and their value and worth in relation to others. Until we understand the social, cultural and historical dynamics - the deeper issues - that make us see unequal, unfair relationships as normal, we will not reach the deeper issues and we cannot hope for more just societies or safer schools.

Who wins/who loses?

We can all be discriminated against for our socioeconomic status, cultural and linguistic diversity, religion, gender, sexuality, disability, ability or personal characteristics, among other factors.

Some individuals and groups lose more than others. Educational disadvantage can be compounded when a student is disadvantaged or discriminated against in more than one way. Members of the dominant cultures may look on bullying incidents such as these as minor, but this is discrimination and it comes from beliefs held in wider society. These beliefs dis-empower and isolate individuals and groups and damage the social harmony of diverse and multicultural Australia.

It is in everyone's - and every group's - interest to understand the deeper issues. We are all likely to take inequity for granted. We may tend to accept that there are no girls on the football field, or that Aboriginal students quit school in the middle of the year, or that the boy in the wheelchair is better off sitting outside the principal's office every lunch time because at least he won't be bullied there.

Everyone loses when unequal power or status is taken for granted. For example, boys convinced that aggressive behaviour demonstrates masculinity are robbed of the relationships skills needed for happiness in adulthood.

Why should school communities know about deeper issues?

Schools are responsible for all their students, but how can all students be safe, respected and included if the status and citizenship of some count for less than others?

Bullying, harassment and discrimination are still part of our social practice. They can represent distrust, fear, misunderstanding, lack of know-ledge or jealousy - all factors that schools can address in positive and active ways.

School communities need to work together to recognise, challenge and change inequalities that fuel bullying and harassment within the school - and to build trust and respect between all groups. By doing this, we are better placed to meet the needs of all students and contribute to a socially just environment.

Creating change

Creating a socially just and equitable school community where everyone is safe, supported and respected requires an integrated approach. This is a coordinated effort that engages and empowers the whole school community in long-term sustainable change while effectively identifying and responding to potential situations and managing specific incidents.

Approaches

Three broad approaches can be combined to suit each school community's situation.

- Collaborative and reflective approaches;
- Behavioural approaches;
- Individual approaches.

Bringing it together

Using behavioural and individual approaches alone is not enough. Reflecting on the issues helps create school communities in which the members feel valued and respected.

Where to now?

Australian school communities are embracing opportunities to talk out, engage with and challenge the issues of bullying, harassment, discrimination and violence. We can see these improvements.

School communities are talking about the issues and developing shared understanding of the underlying factors that maintain these behaviours.

School communities in every state, territory and education sector are designing innovative, local-level, whole-school initiatives.

Legislation and policies are in place that raise awareness of the many forms of harassment and discrimination.

Research is creating an evidence base for action.

But school communities need to be able to tell how their situation is improving and by how much. How can we measure such intangibles as support, trust and acceptance?

Your rights

We all have the right to learn in a safe and supportive school environment that values diversity - an environment free from bullying, harassment, discrimination and violence.

We all have the right to be treated with fairness and dignity.

We all have a responsibility to keep others safe and to treat them in the same way - with fairness, dignity and respect.

I Stop my own bully behaviour

A web page for children entitled *'Get your Angries Out'* is available at http://www.AngriesOut.com. **Lynne Namka** heads the web page that is aimed in part at helping children learn positive ways to deal with their anger. Some of the topics on her web site are:

- Who we are
- For Kids and grownups, too
- Let's learn about bully behaviour
- Helper words for bully behaviour

- Making peace in my world
- When I feel threatened by someone
- My plan for peace
- Breath works
- I stop my own bully behaviour
- Complete bully behaviour curriculum
- For Parents
- For Couples
- Violence in Families
- For Teachers
- I'm sorry I hurt you
- How I stopped my mad attack
- Why did Johnny kill?
- Addictions and co-dependency
- Finding a therapist
- The right man, right woman theory

New Zealand Stop Bullying Guidelines for Schools

(Prepared by Mark Cleary for the New Zealand Police Youth Education Service). Their website: www.nobully.org.nz

Legal requirements...

Schools not only have a moral obligation to reduce bullying, their charter agreement between the school's trustees and the Minister of Education specifically directs the school to *'provide a safe physical and emotional environment'*. (National Administration Guideline Number 5).

The need for an anti-bullying policy

Bullying can be found in every school in the country. It is all too often part of the way young people interact in our society. *Every school must recognise its extent and impact and take steps to stop it happening.* When bullying is ignored or downplayed, pupils will suffer ongoing torment and harassment. It can cause life-long damage to victims. Both bullies and those regularly victimised are more likely to become criminals. A school's failure to deal with bullying endangers the safety of all its pupils by allowing a hostile environment to interfere with learning. *"There is clear, unambiguous evidence that school action can dramatically reduce the incidence of bullying."*

The size of the problem

Scientific studies show that bullying is an international problem that affects all schools. There is a remarkable similarity in the incidence of bullying from country to country, school to school. Bullying knows no international boundaries, socio-economic status or ethnic boundaries.

Few pupils tell a teacher when being bullied (only 20% in one Auckland study - Adair, 1998).

Bullying usually has three common features:

It is a deliberate, hurtful behaviour;

It is repeated;

It is difficult for those being bullied to defend themselves.

There are three main types of bullying:

Physical; hitting, kicking, taking belongings;

Verbal; name-calling, insulting, racist remarks;

Indirect/emotional; spreading nasty stories, excluding from groups.

Bullies

- Are often attention-seekers.
- Will establish their power base by testing the response of the less powerful members of the group, watching how they react when small things happen;
- Find out how the teacher reacts to minor transgressions of the rules and waits to see if the *'victim'* will complain. It is important that teachers are vigilant and consistent;
- Bully because they believe they are popular and have the support of the others;
- Keep bullying because they incorrectly think the behaviour is exciting and makes them popular;
- If there are no consequences to the bad behaviour; if the victim does not complain and if the peer group silently or even actively colludes, the bully will continue with the behaviour.

Victims

- Often have poor social skills;
- Lack the confidence to seek help;
- Don't have the support of the teacher or classmates who find them unappealing;
- Blame themselves and believe it is their own fault;

- Are desperate to *'fit in'*;
- View is very often reinforced by the attitude of adults in their lives
- It is highly unlikely that they will seek help.

Most pupils (80% are not actively involved in bullying. They neither bully nor are victims. They know it's wrong but unless they are asked for help or are made to feel that they have a responsibility or duty to act, they will silently collude with the abuse.

"Every pupil has the <u>right</u> to a safe school and the responsibility to stop bullying."   **Cleary**

Making schools bully free. Taking Immediate Action

Dealing with a bullying incident:

First:

- Express relief that the bullying is now out in the open and can be dealt with.
- Avoid focusing on the shortcomings of the bullying victim.
- Concentrate on where the immediate problem is - the behaviour of the bully.
- The aim of any intervention must be to ***stop the immediate abuse.***
- Ensure that the bully changes his or her behaviour.
- Make the peer group aware and ***ask*** them to help the victim.
- Provide support for the victim
- Ensure the victim has access to a bully-free environment always.
- Use reliable peers, teacher aids, senior volunteers and others as supporters.
- Spend time with the isolated pupil. This can only be a short-term measure as most victims of bullying want to be with their peer group.
- A special safe room that has adequate staff supervision is useful
- Senior students can be used to help run a quiet activities room.

Withdrawn and isolated victims

- Need the opportunity to be involved in special confidence-building programmes.
- Have difficulty integrating with their peer group.

Bullied

- Victim feels withdrawn, passive, shy and introverted.

- When supported victim feels active extroverted, engaged with others.
- Bullied pupils are usually either passive or become so because of the bullying.

1997 Coroner's Report: *"I believe that schools... have a positive duty to be vigilant... to guard against bullying and to deal with it and stamp it out if it occurs. The consequences of a failure to do that can be very profound."*

Change the behaviour of the bully:

Use small group or individual intervention programmes such as:

No Blame Approach. It focuses on seeking the support of the peer group.

The method of **Shared Concern** targets the bully as an individual to accept responsibility before bringing anyone together in a group, including the victim.

Isolate the bullying behaviour

- Remove the bully from the environment; see s/he knows why s/he is being excluded.
- Have the bully reflect on reasons for the isolation.
- Ask the offender to write a letter home explaining why s/he has been isolated
- Check that the letter goes beyond "Because the victim narked on me."

Working with persistent offenders

Some pupils find it difficult to leave behind aggressive ways of relating to other pupils.

The aggression may have been so reinforced that an ongoing programme aimed at developing pro-social skills is necessary. Consider involving Children Young Persons and Their Families Service, Specialist Education Services or other appropriate agency.

In cases of physical assault, involve your local police.

Peer programs

Peer mediation programs have been successful in encouraging young people to seek help when they are in a conflict situation. This may well result in the bully understanding the hurt he/she is causing and modifying their behaviour.

Anti-bullying programs:

Supportive Peers: Accepting of others, empathetic and nice.

Majority: Are looking for leadership

If there's no action:

Bullies: Stay aggressive, nasty and self-centred.

"Successfully dealing with bullying involves building a genuine community within the school. Everyone accepts they have the right to be free from harassment and that they have the responsibility to support their weaker and more vulnerable peers." **Cleary**

What Works Best: A Whole School Approach

Serious international academic studies have found dramatic reductions in bullying of between 20 - 80% when school-wide strategies are used.

The two key messages from these studies are that:

1. *"There is a direct correlation between the time and quality of effort spent in developing a **whole school policy** and the reduction in the levels of bullying"*
2. *"... the process of developing a **common understanding** of the problem is as important as any other factor."*

Stages in the Whole School Approach

There are several clear stages a school needs to go through to become bully-proof or bully-free:

1. **Use a full staff meeting to raise awareness and knowledge of the issue.** The anti-bullying initiative must be tied to the school's philosophy as laid out in the charter. Emphasise the school's statutory obligation to provide a safe environment.
2. A brief presentation to the **Board of Trustees** about **the nature of bullying** will be useful to ensure that the subsequent policy will gain their support and acceptance.
3. **Gather information:**
    a. Find out what similar schools have done.
    b. Survey staff to find out what existing programmes or initiatives in the school complement an anti-bullying approach.
    c. What approach would best fit the current culture of the school?
    d. Develop some base-line data that will give some quantitative information on levels of bullying.

e. Investigate perceptions staff, pupils and parents have about bullying
4. The development of a **'common understanding'** of bullying and expressing this in a *policy* is key to reducing bullying. It must be supported by clear guidelines on how to deal with cases of bullying.
5. **Parent/caregiver meetings** that allow everyone to look at the issues, the nature of the behaviour and the consequence and impact of the bullying on all participants, work well.
6. **Develop advice/information pamphlets.** Personalise the Police/Telecom *'Stop Bullying'* leaflet. Widely advertise the Internet site: http://www.nobully.org.nz and the Freephone (0800 662 855) information line. They contain essential information for at risk pupils.

The immediate problem is the harassment and that is what must be stopped.

Curriculum Action

All pupils in the school will need to have their awareness raised in a variety of ways. This can be:

- Formalised within the curriculum. i.e. taught as part of health/social studies etc.
- Part of special year group training, sessions, or as part of a special pro-social skill development program.

The goal is to sell the idea that:

- Stopping bullying is everyone's responsibility
- Within this, themes need to be carefully developed and reinforced:
- What is bullying?
- Why do people bully?
- Links with other abuse activities.
- Bullying can be stopped!
- Sharing the problem; telling friends, parents and teachers is an essential step.
- Everyone needs to share responsibility to help stop bullying behaviour.
- The problem is the bullying behaviour, not the victim.

There are several options in organising the anti-bullying curriculum and each school needs to choose the approach that is most appropriate for them:
1. Integrating an anti-bullying component into existing curriculum areas.
2. Introducing a series of discrete anti-bullying modules.
3. Anti-bullying modules become part of the health curriculum.
4. Anti-bullying awareness days are held.

Classrooms must always be safe places:

- Free from ridicule, harassment and isolation.
- Where possessions are not stolen or *'borrowed'* by others.
- Where learning takes place in a supportive environment.

Teacher Action

- All staff must be committed to a common response to bullying when it does happen.
- Immediate intervention is crucial.
- Clear procedures must take place when a case of bullying is discovered.
- The school needs to provide necessary support for the individual teacher so that they can maintain a safe classroom environment. The discipline policy and structures are mechanisms to support and maintain safe supportive classrooms.
- There must be clear guidelines that stipulate the responsibilities teaching staff have when dealing with a case of bullying. Everyone needs to accept that his or her classroom must be a safe, supportive environment where bad behaviour is not tolerated, and bullying is recognised, publicly condemned and dealt with.
- Many teachers and schools find it helpful to develop clear statements of what is appropriate behaviour in the classroom.
- This may be in the form of a school-wide **Code of Conduct** or in an individual classroom or school statement.
- Because victims can be passive and withdrawn, others need to tell when they see bullying.
- Good teachers **encourage the 'telling of tales'.** They develop mechanisms to ensure that their pupils can report bad behaviour without fear of retribution or being chastised for telling tales.

A good teacher will:

- Notice when a pupil is isolated and sad.
- Look for the reasons for this.
- Not see it as just play-fighting, name-calling, a bit of fun or just part of growing up.
- Work with the victim to stop the offending behaviour.
- Not tell the victim to ignore it, to sort it out themselves or to hit back.

"Teachers must recognise that a safe classroom is the most effective way of developing a positive learning environment." **Cleary**

Pupil Action

Schools will develop a **'telling environment'** when they gain pupil trust and support.

If pupils know that the telling will result in a fair resolution they will trust the adults with information about bad behaviour.

This environment can be supported by constant attention to:

- Basic codes of behaviour.
- The maintenance of a co-operative, well-ordered, tolerant classroom

When pupils can tell, without attracting the attention of offending peers. Where their actions are affirmed by the teacher taking appropriate action.

Senior pupils may play a vital role in many anti-bullying activities. They can fulfil a very important role by providing non-threatening contacts. Use them in drama role-plays and during curriculum discussions on bullying.

Outside the classroom:

- The *'active'* nature of most bullies makes it very important that free time is well supervised and that there are plenty of opportunities for them to be kept busy.
- Have as many activities as possible available with clear rules to avoid the minority dominating.
- Ensure that pupils who feel vulnerable, or who are currently in a bully-victim relationship, have a safe place to go.
- Survey pupils as to the places and times they may feel vulnerable or not safe.

- Provide adequate supervision in places and times that pupils identify.
- Target areas and activities where bullies dominate. Introduce activities that will involve the bullies and encourage them to participate positively.
- Have discipline procedures in place that isolate the bad behaviour by removing the persistent offenders from the environment.
- Monitor the movement of pupils around the campus between classes. Their arrival and departure from school and what they can do at lunchtime are important issues.
- Young people are searching for leadership, support and clarification from the adults in the school.

Chapter 11

HOW TO PREVENT AND STOP SCHOOL BULLYING

UNITED KINGDOM

Using humour

Pelswick is a 13-year-old eighth grader who lives with dad Quentin, sister Kate and Gram-Gram. He's in a wheelchair because his legs are paralysed but this never stops Pelswick enjoying himself - although it can cause a few problems when the school bullies decide it's his turn to be picked on. Luckily, Pelswick is a lot brighter than them and is never short of a smart remark to stop them in their tracks. When one bully calls him a *'cripple'* he quips that he prefers the term *'permanently seated'!*

Bullying - Don't Suffer in Silence. An anti-bullying pack for schools.

(Based on recent research, relevant experience, and current legislation - co-ordinated by **Professor Peter Smith**, Goldsmith's College University of London. Crown Copyright 2000, produced by the Department of Education and Employment on behalf of government.) www.dfes.gov.uk/bullying

The government attempt to paper over the cracks - this time it's a drive to reduce expulsion figures by coercing schools to keep bullies in school rather than expel them - has, as expected, backfired. Head teachers now warn that any school that keeps its bullies in lessons might be prosecuted under the Human Rights Act for allowing pupils to be subjected to degrading treatment. In an apparent U-turn, the government's latest school information pack called *"Don't suffer in Silence"* states, *"It should be clear what the sanctions are for bullying and in what circumstances they will apply. Strong sanctions such as exclusion may be necessary in cases of severe bullying."* Alas, this will only move the bullies to somewhere else. Is there no one at DfEE who can understand that bullying needs to be tackled at source?

The Department has updated the December 2000 edition of the Pack *'Bullying: don't suffer in Silence'* (0064/2000) in September 2002 and hard copies are available free of charge from: Produced by the

Department for Education and Employment. Copies available from **DfES Publications in Nottingham on 0845 602 2260.**

Stephen Twigg MP says, "All schools should now have an anti-bullying policy and I know most take the issue very seriously. Indeed, this pack was produced in response to a demand from schools and put together with the help and advice of many teachers.

Most recent figures show that over 20,000 calls were made to **Childline** about bullying last year. That's 17 per cent of all their calls and the single most frequently cited issue. Clearly, we all have a duty to these children to ensure they feel safe, secure and valued."

Bullying hurts and you don't have to endure it. If you are on the receiving end of bullying, there are many things that can be done to make your life easier. This web site is intended to show pupils, their families and teachers how to tackle a problem that has gone on for far too long.

It is packed with new ideas, practical techniques and the valuable experiences of those who have been bullied, or have even bullied others, to demonstrate that *you need not Suffer in Silence*.

Don't Suffer in Silence Study

The following three case studies provide further reading to accompany the DfEE anti-bullying pack, **Don't Suffer in Silence**. They feature a primary school and two secondary schools which, in various ways, are committed to reducing bullying. They are not presented as *'ideal'* types, but as realistic examples of progress made, and difficulties experienced.

Example 1:

A study was conducted in a medium-sized primary school employing twelve teaching staff and one part-time support teacher. Pupils come from a restricted catchment area in the centre of a large town. A fairly large proportion of pupils come from single parent families, and unemployment in the area is higher than the town's average.

In 1994 the head teacher reported an increase in disruptive and anti-social behaviour over his ten years at the school. He was particularly concerned about what he perceived to be an increase in physical bullying and intimidation, especially since it was not restricted to just a few pupils. He spoke of *'a culture of bullying'* that in his view reflected some sections of the local community. He pointed to vandalism of the school building as evidence of an anti-social ethos in some of the local youths.

In 1995, one of the teachers (the co-ordinating teacher) attended a seminar on anti-bullying initiatives and, with the support of the head teacher, set about co-ordinating the development of a formal whole-school anti-bullying policy and exploring other interventions. A questionnaire survey of the entire school showed almost half the pupils had been bullied *'sometimes'* or more often, and about a quarter reported they had bullied, in the current term. These high figures alarmed the head teacher and so bullying became a key issue he wanted addressed.

A special meeting of teaching staff in late 1995 was led by the co-ordinating teacher and an invited anti-bullying researcher. A consensus was that a whole-school policy should be the key response and that other more specific actions should follow and link up with the policy. It was decided to offer lunchtime supervisors the chance to attend a whole-day training course, to train teachers how to work with pupils involved in bullying, and that teachers would tackle bullying in class.

As part of the awareness-raising exercise and as a way of including all people connected with the school, a series of meetings were held in 1996. The head teacher also arranged for a special meeting to which parents were invited but few attended. Teachers and pupils fed their ideas to the co-ordinating teacher who then, in collaboration with the head teacher, produced a first draft. This provided a definition of bullying, a statement that made clear why bullying would not be tolerated in the school, what sanctions would follow if a pupil was found to be bullying, and guidelines on what action should be taken if someone experienced bullying. It was circulated to all pupils and teaching staff and to parents with requests for comments and suggestions.

These views were considered by the head teacher and the co-ordinating teacher and a final version produced in May 1996. The policy was announced at an assembly and copies posted on every classroom wall and throughout the school. Each class discussed bullying and the policy in the launch week.

From the launch of the policy through to the end of that school year, all class teachers reported that they had raised bullying as an issue with their pupils. Some continued to do so when reports of bullying came to their attention. In the following academic year, some teachers, especially of the older grades, carried out more systematic work that included the Quality Circle approach, story writing, drama, and literature (such as Ronald Dahl's *Rhyme Stew* and *The Twits*).

Part way through the 1996/97 school year the co-ordinating teacher was approached by some of the school's lunchtime supervisors who expressed concerns about *'being left out'* of the anti-bullying work. They complained that the head teacher had informed them some time ago that they were to have an opportunity to attend a training course but that they had heard nothing since then. The co-ordinating teacher also reported that several teachers believed that the lunchtime supervisors sometimes acted in ways that were inconsistent with the stated policy about how the school would respond to bullying. It became clear that the lunchtime supervisors felt devalued in the school and that they wanted to play a more active role in the school's anti-bullying initiatives. At a meeting with the head teacher it was agreed that the training course would run early in the following school year.

The lunchtime supervisors attended a one-day training course and shared and acquired basic knowledge about bullying. The facilitator challenged some myths about bullying and how it should be responded to, and this led some of the supervisors to change how they defined bullying.

Other activities focused on preventive strategies (such as regular patrols of *'bullying hot spot'* and keeping a close watch on pupils known to be vulnerable to being picked on) and how the difference between bullying and playful fighting could be distinguished.

The head teacher was very impressed with the lunchtime supervisors' role in helping to prevent and respond to bullying. He reported a fall in the number of pupils sent to him for misbehaving during lunch breaks. The supervisors attributed this to their greater confidence in dealing with bullying. One said that, *"I no longer let the children hide behind the excuse that they were only playing. I now have ways to convince myself that this really is or isn't the case."*

The questionnaire survey has been repeated twice. Despite a slow reduction in bullying at the start of the project, the final survey suggested that the figures had reduced to about one in ten pupils for both bullying and being bullied. Although still high, most of these cases involved *'low level'* bullying such as disputes between friends that are quickly resolved. Moreover, there has been a huge decrease in levels of physical bullying (down from 46% in the first survey to 5% in the final survey).

The co-ordinating teacher left the school at the end of the 1996-97 school year. No other teacher was willing to take up this role. However, the head teacher recognised the benefits that the actions taken so far had brought about and so decided to *'lead from the front'*.

The second survey, about 18 months after the first, showed a reduction in being bullied (down to 38%) and bullying others (down to 18%) - still very high. Moreover, many pupils reported a shift in being bullied from the school premises to the journey home in the afternoon. When the head teacher became aware of this shift, he arranged for it to be raised as an issue in assemblies and in the classroom. Further, it led to a change to the wording of the whole-school policy to make it clear that all bullying was unacceptable among its members regardless of where this took place.

The co-ordinating teacher had been due to tell colleagues what she had learned through attending training courses. However, she left the school before being able to do so. The head teacher was unable to fund this type of training for the remaining staff, so the school was not able to add this type of intervention to its list of actions.

Summary

Before intervening, a very high proportion of pupils were involved in bullying, particularly physical assaults and intimidation. Range of actions taken including developing a whole-school policy, curriculum/classroom work, and training of lunchtime supervisors. Intervention suffered loss of momentum when co-ordinating teacher left school. Head teacher continued to support anti-bullying activity. Large reductions in incidence of bullying, especially physical bullying.

Example 2:

This secondary school has over 1200 pupils aged 11-18 years and 67.5 teaching staff. In many ways its actions to combat bullying could be considered proactive rather than reactive.

Work began at a time when bullying was not a major issue in the school, but a consensus was emerging among several people, particularly the school counsellor, the pastoral deputy head and the head teacher, about the sort of social climate they envisaged. This was to be based on the counselling model of a *'sharing approach'* to the whole school community, placing relationships at the heart of curricular and pastoral work. The whole-school anti-bullying policy was developed to be an aspect of a wider whole-school equal opportunities policy.

The school decided it wanted to adopt a long term and co-ordinated approach, with all other interventions designed to be part of an overarching framework. Initiatives included a comprehensive peer support scheme, contracting by pupils and their parents, PSHE work that focused on issues around bullying, and curriculum activities where appropriate. As evidence for the school's high level of commitment to addressing the problem, an anti-bullying working party was set up almost at the outset with representatives from teaching and non-teaching staff and pupils.

A whole-school approach quickly led to a whole-school day workshop which raised awareness of bullying and created a consensus about the actions to be taken to address it - co-ordinated by the anti-bullying working party.

The policy was drafted in 1991 and it remained a draft for four years. Nevertheless, it continued to be viewed positively by pupils, parents and staff. In 1995, the anti-bullying working party formalised it into a short-written statement. This contained the school's definition of bullying, current practice and clarified directions for the future.

The written policy was published in the staff handbook and posted throughout the school building. Although the anti-bullying working party continued to operate, two members of staff - the pastoral deputy head and the school counsellor - were instrumental in ensuring that the specific anti-bullying actions identified during the whole-school day workshop were realised.

A Pupil Helper Scheme built upon the work carried out by the school counsellor that began in 1984. This early work taught volunteers from Years 11, 12 and 13 how to use the Re-evaluation Counselling model. Since the scheme became part of the overall anti-bullying policy, more emphasis was given to helping the peer counsellors listen to and support those involved in bullying. Formal training by the school counsellor was augmented by self-development by co-counselling among the volunteers. Uptake of this initiative has been high - around 50 pupils a year since 1992 have become pupil helpers. The training they receive is cascaded down to the younger pupils as they regularly spend time in tutor periods, teaching listening and co-counselling skills, and running self-esteem-building activities and quality circles.

All pupils have opportunities for individual time with peer helpers and they are offered the choice to see a teacher or a pupil counsellor. Alongside this formal *'booking'* arrangement, there is also a lunchtime drop-in facility. An important aspect of the scheme is that it has made clear that pupil helpers are not responsible for managing bullying. They receive regular adult supervision and support and, most crucially, they offer users limited confidentiality. In cases of extreme bullying they have a duty of disclosure to an adult member of staff.

An anti-bullying contract is introduced to all pupils in Year 7. They voted on the form and wording of the contract and this was acknowledged in the contract itself, along with three principles that pupils agreed to follow. These were:

(i) treat fellow pupils with respect;
(ii) don't humiliate or hurt others physically or verbally; and
(iii) help others who are being hurt or upset through bullying.

Parents are also asked to sign, to confirm that they will strive to ensure that their child abides by it. The contract is discussed in PSHE classes so that each pupil can appreciate how seriously it is taken.

Surveys have been carried out at regular intervals, involving questionnaires and pupil and staff interviews. Instances of bullying are also recorded by heads of year.

The school regards the increased tendency of pupils to report being bullied as a success, especially as this trend has been accompanied by a four-fold reduction in *'serious'* cases - now down to around one a month. There has also been a reduction in pupils reporting that they have been involved in, or witnessed, bullying. Pupils' written responses suggest they are not as prepared as before to accept bullying. When they do report it, pupils generally believe it is dealt with effectively. In general, they regard the school as *'taking bullying very seriously'*.

The school recognises it has taken quite a time for some members of staff to commit themselves to the anti-bullying policy. One reason may have been that it was initiated and driven by a handful of colleagues at first. Another is that some staff may not have recognised that bullying needed to be addressed.

Although the school recognises that they have largely broken the culture of silence that so often surrounds bullying, they have been faced with the need to spend more time dealing with both serious and minor instances. Teachers are encouraged to be patient and not abruptly to dismiss pupils reporting apparently trivial incidents. Because of the greater awareness but decreased tolerance of bullying some pupils have adopted more subtle forms of abuse, particularly verbal.

Summary

- A concerted and co-ordinated approach was proactive rather than reactive;
- Effective use of anti-bullying working party;
- Peer helper scheme integrated with policy work;
- Greater awareness, and reduced tolerance, of bullying; and
- Decrease in general and serious bullying.

Example 3:

This mixed comprehensive school has some 450, 11-16-year-old pupils taught by 30 teachers. It serves a disadvantaged city district. 63% of the pupils are eligible for free school meals; 60% are from single parent families; 40% are on the school's special educational needs register.

The school has a well-articulated code of conduct and an equal opportunities policy that specifies its expectations about pupils' behaviour, including bullying. Copies of these documents are given to all pupils when they join the school, and to their parents. The school's Anti-Bullying Campaign (ABC) peer support system is an integral part of the way in which the code of conduct and the equal opportunities policy are implemented in practice. The anti-bullying work in the school was established after careful planning and consultation with all interested groups. It has strong support from the school's governors, senior managers, and most of the teachers, parents and pupils who are all well informed about the system.

ABC involves pupil peer supporters trained to offer help to other pupils who are being bullied. Some of the peer supporters visit the school's feeder primaries where they speak to prospective pupils and their parents about the school's ABC scheme. These visits are re-enforced early in the school year when all new pupils (Year 7) have a series of PSHE lessons on the code of conduct including the school's anti-bullying stance and what victims can do if they are bullied. Bullying and the ABC system are also frequent topics of assemblies for all year groups of pupils.

This peer support system was established because of concern that bullying was going unreported, despite appeals to speak up - and pupils had thought adults would not understand. However, it is not intended to replace any of the people to whom victims might report their bullying problems; it is simply another avenue that they may use.

Consultation meetings with the school's senior managers, teachers, ancillary staff and some of the pupils were positive and the system was established in 1996. A teacher has day-to-day responsibility for managing, administering and monitoring it under the oversight of the other teacher, a deputy head.

Prospective peer supporters from Year 8 and above are invited to complete an application form. The short-listed applicants are interviewed by the educational psychologist, the counsellor and existing peer supporters, based on how convincingly the forms have been completed. A history of bad behaviour is not in itself a reason for excluding a pupil from consideration. *"I'm clear in my own mind that you're aiming to recruit the kids...who've got big 'cred,' are shiny, attractive and who people will think that if they're doing it then it must be a good thing. Often, they'll be a bit naughty, but you need the 'cred' that they bring with them"* (Educational psychologist). Unusually, for many mixed-sex schools that have a peer support system, this school has succeeded in achieving a gender balance amongst the peer supporters. Successful interviewees are invited to attend extensive training sessions run by the school counsellor and the educational psychologist. Only on the successful completion of this training are individual interviewees appointed as peer supporters.

Lunchtime group supervision meetings, lasting for 30 minutes, are run every week by at least two of the adults. Unnamed individual cases are discussed, during which supporters occasionally seek advice and disseminate ideas on, for example, appropriate or successful approaches.

The teacher in charge of the ABC system conducts an annual anonymous questionnaire survey of all the pupils and teachers in the school. In 1997, 39 per cent of pupil respondents said they had ever *'been a bully in this school'*. For 1998 and 1999, the corresponding figures were 41 and 30 per cent respectively. There has also been a decline in the number of pupil respondents who report having ever *'been bullied in this school'*. In 1997, 58 per cent did so, whilst the corresponding figures for 1998 and 1999 were 53 and 42 per cent respectively.

At the end of the 1997 autumn term, unnamed records showed the system had dealt with forty-seven cases involving sixty-two pupil victims since the service began in mid-1996. Apparently, the anti-bullying work has encouraged pupils to tell someone they are being bullied, as well as reducing the numbers of bullies and victims.

Summary

- Well integrated peer support system with wide support;
- System managed by a co-operative team of adults with clearly defined roles and who are careful in the selection, training and super-vision of the peer supporters;
- System has a clearly defined function, understood by peer supporters and users;
- Regular evaluation through questionnaire surveys and analysis of records;
- Progress in encouraging use of the peer support service and in reducing bullying.

Comparison of the three examples:

These schools were not in privileged positions. Schools 1 and 3 had many pupils from disadvantaged backgrounds. All three schools took bullying seriously and brought in outside help early on - getting strong support from the head teacher or senior management, and consultation on how to proceed. Responsibilities were also clearly assigned.

In all three schools the approach has centred around a whole school policy; but the emphasis of the work has varied. School 1, a primary school, put a lot of emphasis on the playground, training of lunchtime supervisors, and curriculum work. Schools 2 and 3 both used peer support or helper schemes as a central approach. In each case these methods were carefully planned and integrated with the policy and other methods.

These schools also faced difficulties, such as changes in key staff, resentments, and sometimes scepticism from parents, governors or even teaching staff that bullying needed to be addressed seriously, or that a proposed method was appropriate. It is likely that in any sustained initiative difficulties will be encountered, but these schools persevered in their efforts.

Each school has successes to report, sometimes immediate, sometimes after a short-term rise in reporting (school 3) as the topic is 'opened up,' followed by a fall. Bullying is far from being eliminated in these schools, but the planned and concerted efforts are clearly having a positive impact.

Child Bullying - School Bullying, Bullyside UK National Workplace Bullying Advice Line [Tim Field]

Each year, at least 16 children kill themselves in the UK because they are being bullied at school and no one in authority is doing anything to tackle the bullying. Failure by a school to implement an effective, active anti-bullying policy is a breach of duty of care.

From 1 September 1999, all UK schools are legally required to have an anti-bullying policy.

Selecting a safe school for your child

When selecting a school for your child, avoid any school where there is no anti-bullying policy and especially where the staff or head claims, "We don't need an anti-bullying policy, there's no bullying here." It is in these schools that bullying is most prevalent. If the school has an anti-bullying policy, check that it's effective; some schools have a policy as a window-dressing exercise. A policy is only words on paper; its effectiveness is in the commitment of the head teacher or principal. Ask the experts: talk to the pupils and ex-pupils in private and in confidence. Talk to the children who are artistic, gifted, of high integrity and non-aggressive - these are the ones most likely to be targeted by bullies.

Bullies are people who act outside the bounds of society and will regard the absence of an anti-bullying policy, or failure to implement a policy effectively, as encouragement and approval of their antisocial behaviour.

When judging which school is likely to be best for your child, don't be fooled by league tables; these show only exam results (called 'standards' by OFSTED and the DfEE) which are only one aspect of school life. Remember that academic exam results are one of the least reliable indicators of potential and that many of the world's most successful people (i.e. Albert Einstein [physics], Soichira Honda [Honda Motor Corporation], Ray Kroc [founder of MacDonalds]) left school with few or no qualifications.

To find out what a school is really like, ask for the following figures for the last academic year:

- Rate of staff turnover

- Amount of staff sick leave
- Number of days when supply staff are engaged
- Number of different supply staff engaged
- Number of stress breakdowns of staff
- Number of suicides and attempted suicides amongst staff
- Number of suicides and attempted suicides amongst pupils
- Number of ill-health retirements
- Number of early retirements
- Number of grievances started
- Number of uses of disciplinary procedures (verbal and written warnings issued)
- Number of suspensions of staff
- Number of dismissals of staff
- Number of times the employer is involved in employment tribunals or legal action against employees
- Attendance record of pupils
- Number of pupil exclusions
- Amount of damage to school property including graffiti
- Presence of an anti-bullying policy
- Views of the pupils, especially past pupils

The figures will also give you a good indication to how wisely your council tax and other taxes are being spent. Bullying prevents all children in the class from undertaking their studies; exam results will be lower than they could and should be.

SCOTLAND

The *Anti-Bullying Network* web site (www.antibullying.net), funded by the Scottish Executive is on line. *Andrew Mellor*, Network Manager, said the project pulls together experience and advice on identifying and tackling bullying.

In a proactive move, the Law Society of Scotland distributed leaflets throughout Scotland advising children of their legal rights and that they don't have to put up with bullying. The leaflets also provide information for adults being abused at home or bullied at work. This action follows Edinburgh City council's instruction that all schools in the city must record incidents of racism and bullying.

Chapter 12

HOW TO PREVENT AND STOP SCHOOL BULLYING USA, CANADA and THE NETHERLANDS

UNITED STATES

Take a Stand Program (USA): Prevention of bullying and interpersonal violence

(This program is advocated for Kindergarten - Grade 5, parents and teachers:)

Bullying is something most children encounter in one form or another. Children struggle with being called names, being picked upon, being excluded, not knowing how to make friends, or being the ones acting unkindly or aggressively toward others. All forms of bullying are abusive, and all are opportunities to teach children how to get along, how to be considerate people, how to be part of a community or group.

The **Take a Stand Program** is a revolutionary approach to prevention of bullying. Starting at the Kindergarten level and progressing through Grade 5, children learn about bullying, its effects, how to stop it and the importance of mutual acceptance and respect.

For the first time, schools, churches, youth groups, after school programs, etc. have a tool to teach all children how to be advocates for creating a community that will not tolerate bullying behaviours; to teach children who are bullied how to stand up for themselves; and to teach the bullies themselves alternate ways of handling their own feelings of not belonging.

At the same time, teachers, school administrators and parents learn that it is possible to **Take a Stand** for having a community that will not tolerate bullying. For too long, adults have believed that bullying is just part of growing up, that there have always been kids who are jocks and kids who are geeks; those who are *'in'* and those who are *'out'*. This acceptance has prevented adults from stopping this pattern.

The Take a Stand Program challenges this acceptance from the earliest possible age, creating a new standard for interpersonal relationships. Just as children led the drive to use seatbelts and to reduce smoking, they are leaders in setting a new course for how we treat one another.

The Take a Stand Program creates a school-wide community of interpersonal problem solving and mutual respect that has been embraced by school administrators, teachers, parents and children. If you would like this Program to be a part of your children's education, please share this information with your school, youth group or Parent Teacher organization.

Dr. Sherryll Kraizer, author of the Take a Stand Program (for children in kindergarten to grade 5), has a Ph.D. in Education with a specialization in youth at risk. She is also the author of the ***Safe Child Program for the Prevention of Child Abuse;*** (Preschool - Grade 3, parents and teachers); the ***Reach*** (Grade 1 to 6) and ***Challenge*** (Grades 7 to 12) programs for at-risk youth; the ***Recovery Program*** (Grade 1 to adult) for previously victimized children; and a ***Prevention of Dating Violence Program.*** Dr. Kraizer is internationally recognized for her prevention programs and creating models for maximizing community-wide participation in prevention effectiveness. They can be ordered by bringing up her web page: www.safechild.org or through the Coalition for Children in Denver Colorado.

State of New Jersey Anti-bullying Legislation

An Act concerning the adoption of harassment and bullying prevention policies by public school districts and supplementing chapter 37 of Title 18A of the New Jersey Statutes as adopted by the Senate Education Committee. (This is an excellent example on how to implement and enforce policies against school bullying).

Be It Enacted by the Senate and General Assembly of the State of New Jersey:

1. The Legislature finds and declares that: a safe and civil environment in school is necessary for students to learn and achieve high academic standards; harassment, intimidation or bullying, like other disruptive or violent behaviours, is conduct that disrupts both a student's ability to learn and a school's ability to educate its students in a safe environment; and since students learn by example, school administrators, faculty, staff, and volunteers should be commended for demonstrating appropriate

behaviour, treating others with civility and respect, and refusing to tolerate harassment, intimidation or bullying.
2. As used in this act: *'Harassment, intimidation or bullying'* means any gesture or written, verbal or physical act that is reasonably perceived as being motivated either by any actual or perceived characteristic, such as race, colour, religion, ancestry, national origin, gender, sexual orientation, gender identity and expression, or a mental, physical or sensory handicap, or by any other distinguishing characteristic, that takes place on school property, at any school-sponsored function or on a school bus and that:
   a. A reasonable person should know, under the circumstances, will have the effect of harming a student or damaging the student's property, or placing a student in reasonable fear of harm to his person or damage to his property; or
   b. Has the effect of insulting or demeaning any student or group of students in such a way as to cause substantial disruption in, or substantial interference with, the orderly operation of the school.
3. a. Each school district shall adopt a policy prohibiting harassment, intimidation or bullying on school property, at a school-sponsored function or on a school bus. The school district shall attempt to adopt the policy through a process that includes representation of parents or guardians, school employees, volunteers, students, administrators, and community representatives.
   b. A school district shall have local control over the content of the policy, except that the policy shall contain, at a minimum, the following components:
1. a statement prohibiting harassment, intimidation or bullying of a student;
2. a definition of harassment, intimidation or bullying no less inclusive than that set forth in section 2 of this act;
3. a description of the type of behaviour expected from each student;
4. consequences and appropriate remedial action for a person who commits an act of harassment, intimidation or bullying;
5. a procedure for reporting an act of harassment, intimidation or bullying, including a provision that permits a person to report an act of harassment, intimidation or bullying anonymously; however, this shall not be construed to permit formal disciplinary action solely based on an anonymous report;

6. a procedure for prompt investigation of reports of violations and complaints, identifying either the principal or the principal's designee as the person responsible for the investigation; the range of ways in which a school will respond once an incident of harassment, intimidation or bullying is identified;
7. a statement that prohibits reprisal or retaliation against any person who reports an act of harassment, intimidation or bullying and the consequence and appropriate remedial action for a person who engages in reprisal or retaliation;
8. consequences and appropriate remedial action for a person found to have falsely accused another as a means of retaliation or as a means of harassment, intimidation or bullying; and
9. a statement of how the policy is to be publicized, including notice that the policy applies to participation in school-sponsored functions.
10. A school district shall adopt a policy and transmit a copy of its policy to the appropriate county superintendent of schools by September 1, 2003.
11. To assist school districts in developing policies for the prevention of harassment, intimidation or bullying, the Commissioner of Education shall develop a model policy applicable to grades kindergarten through year 12. This model policy shall be issued no later than December 1, 2002.
12. Notice of the school district's policy shall appear in any publication of the school district that sets forth the comprehensive rules, procedures and standards of conduct for schools within the school district, and in any student handbook.
13. a. A school employee, student or volunteer shall not engage in reprisal, retaliation or false accusation against a victim, witness or one with reliable information about an act of harassment, intimidation or bullying.
    b. A school employee, student or volunteer who has witnessed, or has reliable information that a student has been subject to, harassment, intimidation or bullying shall report the incident to the appropriate school official designated by the school district's policy.
    c. A school employee who promptly reports an incident of harassment, intimidation or bullying, to the appropriate school official designated by the school district's policy, and who makes this report in compliance with the procedures in the district's

Dealing with School Bullying

policy, is immune from a cause of action for damages arising from any failure to remedy the reported incident.
14. a. Schools and school districts are encouraged to establish bullying prevention programs, and other initiatives involving school staff, students, administrators, volunteers, parents, law enforcement and community members.
    b. To the extent funds are appropriated for these purposes, a school district shall:
    i. provide training on the school district's harassment, intimidation or bullying policies to school employees and volunteers who have significant contact with students; and
    ii. develop a process for discussing the district's harassment, intimidation or bullying policy with students.
    c. Information regarding the school district policy against harassment, intimidation or bullying shall be incorporated into a school's employee training program.
15. This act shall not be interpreted to prevent a victim from seeking redress under any other available law either civil or criminal. This act does not create or alter any tort liability.
16. A school district that incurs additional costs due to the implementation of the provisions of this act shall apply to the Commissioner of Education for reimbursement.
17. This act shall take effect immediately.

CANADA

School Resources Officers - Edmonton Police Services

The 2002/03 school year is the 23rd anniversary of the School Resource Officer Program. In 1979, the Edmonton Police Service entered into a unique partnership with the Edmonton Public and Edmonton Separate School Boards. The basis for this uniqueness is the innovative nature of creating a police presence within four Edmonton high schools. The program has grown to include 12 sworn police officers, working solely out of offices in 15 different Edmonton high schools. ***The School Resource Officer Program*** is still recognized as one of the first community-based initiatives undertaken by the EPS.

Over the past 20 years, the role of the School Resource Officer has changed dramatically. A primary function of these members today, is to ensure a *'safe and caring place of learning'*. In addition to being an active participant of the school administrative team, the School

Resource Officer must create and find balances between law enforcer, school administrator, teacher, friend, coach, and counsellor.

The School Resource Officer Unit can be a very rewarding experience for the members assigned, as friendships develop over the years with both students and staff. The position provides opportunities to develop strong leadership and administrative skills, along with superior time management, public speaking, and coaching skills. It is community policing in its purist form.

S.A.R.A. program - Edmonton Police Services

(Prepared by Cst. Rick Cole)

Police officers speak at schools explaining the consequences of bullying. They also address the students about the unacceptability of standing by when they observe bullying - that they must stop it or at least report it. No longer is it acceptable to either bully or stand by and watch it happening.

Students who get into fights at school sign a contract with the police officer, the school and the parents involved that they will straighten out, otherwise they'll be charged by the police. Others sign contracts that they will do their homework, behave at home and write a paper about being assertive without being violent.

One last resort for parents is to contemplate getting the police involved by lodging assault charges against the bully. Often having a police officer reprimand the bully, will result in positive changes in the bully's behaviour. Do everything you can, before resorting to changing schools for your child.

The S.A.R.A. program was prepared by Constable R. Cole of the Edmonton Police Services in Alberta, Canada. He explained that in the police world a child is somebody under the age of 12 and the word youth means person 12 to 18 years old. He works with people in both age groups, so he chose the word kid to describe both groups:

"In early November 1998 I arrested a 14-year-old boy for shoplifting at the Bay in West Edmonton Mall. This was the youth's first contact with the police. I completed my report and recommended him for the Alternative Measures Program."

In February 1999 I arrested the same youth for shoplifting in West Edmonton Mall. I asked the youth about his Alternative Measures and why he was anxious to test the court system. The youth's reply was simple: *"I have not heard anything from Alternative Measures. It doesn't matter because nothing happens when you get caught."*

This statement stayed with me in all my future dealings with young offenders. A short time later I had dealings with another 14-year-old, first time offender. The youth had been arrested inside a vehicle he was trying to steal, by the owner of the vehicle. The youth claimed he had been assaulted by the vehicle owner because *"he held me and would not let me go."* The youth claimed he knew his rights. This was the youth's first contact with police. I completed my report and recommended the youth to the Alternative Measures Program. The youth was more concerned about the actions of the vehicle owner than his own. The youth felt his actions did not matter because he was a kid.

In March 1999 I was sent to investigate a noise complaint. The noise was being caused by a mother/daughter shouting match. Mom was angry with her 13-year-old daughter because her daughter had stayed out all night. The mother did not know where her daughter had been as she did not have permission to be out. According to Mom, the daughter had been acting out and was totally defiant at home, had not been attending school, and the mother did not know what to do. The daughter felt the argument meant nothing and Mom would let it blow over the same way arguments always did.

A couple of months later, the daughter was turned over to me by Security at West Edmonton Mall. She was arrested in the company of four boys who were responsible for starting a fire in the mall.

The daughter was high on cocaine. She had not committed a convictable offence and admitted to doing nothing. She was not a candidate for Alternative Measures.

My patrol duties took me into several different schools. The schools presented students to me that had committed a wide range of offences. These problem students had displayed troubles that ranged between criminal offences and discipline troubles. The students ranged in ages from 10 to 18 years. Their issues included:

1. bullying
2. assaults
3. thefts
4. skipping (poor attendance)
5. swearing and disrespect
6. disruptive behaviour and conduct

7. mischief
8. gang involvement
9. racial tensions
10. being abused and neglected kids.

These youth's crimes had already exhausted most methods of discipline available to the schools. The youths knew the rules and felt nothing could be done to them. For many of the youths I encountered in the school, this was their first contact with the police. A small percentage of these troubled youths had committed convictable offences and satisfied the requirements for a recommendation to the Alternative Measures Program. I believe the problem presented to me in my dealings with first time offending young people involved three parts.

The first of the three parts involves the simple *'gap'* in time between apprehension or first contact with police, and the time of initial contact by staff from the Alternative Measures Program. This time *'gap'* can be anywhere from three weeks to six months. A month is a lifetime for a 12-year-old and for consequences to be effective they need to occur in a timely manner.

The second part of this equation involves the nature of the consequences themselves. Consequences need to provide a real or meaningful punishment suitable for the offence. Consequences also need to provide an educational or problem-solving component. The young offender needs to be shown how to change the inappropriate behaviour in a safe, positive way. The Alternative Measures Program is outstanding at finding meaningful punishment. Unfortunately, this still leaves a *'gap'* in the second part of effective consequences.

The final part of the problem arises when the youth has not committed a convictable offence and cannot be recommended to the Alternative Measures Program. We know some of these children will straighten themselves out and there will be no role to be played by the police. We also know some of these children are in real crisis and to do nothing means we will be arresting them in the future.

My experience in dealing with first time offenders revealed there is a *'gap'* in the system. We are doing a disservice to our youth by not filling it.

The *'gap'* was initially believed to be the result of the system itself. The offender was arrested by the police and subsequently released to a parent. The offender took responsibility for committing the offence.

The police recommended the youth to the Alternative Measures Program. The Alternative Measures Program is administered by the Prosecutor's Office, which is a separate provincial agency operated outside the police agency.

The entire process takes time. The police report needs to be written, approved, and forwarded to court liaison section. Court liaison then forwards the report to the Crown's office, where it is read. Finally, the report is processed and delivered to a staff member in the Alternative Measures office. The staff member drafts a letter that is delivered to the offender and his parent, establishing initial contact from the Alternative Measures Program. This process takes a minimum of three weeks and can take as long as six months, depending on numbers.

This time delay can make the punishment irrelevant to the offence in the mind of a young person. The intent of the Alternative Measures program is excellent. Problems arise because of the lag time caused by processing reports. The offender does not perceive the consequences as real or meaningful. Unfortunately, this leads to the misconception that the offender is not accountable for his actions.

A second *'gap'* appeared when initially dealing with the offender. The offenders expressed a belief that they had *'rights'* because they were young offenders, and property owners could not hold them accountable. Some offenders showed no respect for the victims. It was okay to take something because it was *'there'*.

This lack of respect really hit home when I dealt with the offender captured inside a vehicle by the vehicle owner. In this case the vehicle owner was a huge, powerful man and the offender an average-sized 14-year-old boy. The vehicle owner did not administer any abusive punishment prior to police arrival. The man simply held the boy by the arm, preventing him from running away.

The offender was turned over to me without any injury. The offender alleged all sorts of things and initially denied being in the vehicle. He said he had been punched and kicked and beaten up. The offender demanded the vehicle owner be arrested because the offender was only 14 and he had rights. The offender was arrested and taken to a police station and allowed to call a lawyer and his mom. The lawyer, in return, spoke to me and wanted to know if Alternative Measures could be an option. I explained all the requirements for a recommendation to the program had not been met. The lawyer and the offender spoke again. The offender said he was sorry and admitted his part in the occurrence. It was clear the offender had to be released with a recommendation to the Alternative Measures Program, but it was also clear that the offender was playing the system to avoid consequences.

The system was established to help young offenders develop into valued citizens, but in some cases the young offenders were using the system to support their crimes against citizens.

The last *'gap'* in the system was most apparent when I visited young people at school. This difficulty arose because the actions of the youth had not crossed the line into becoming a criminal offence. The gap at this level is huge. Schools, parents and social services identify at risk children. These youths act out by skipping school, fighting, bullying and disrespecting authorities. Parents are at a loss as to what to do next. Schools and Social Services have exhausted the punitive actions they have access to. The youths have learned how to manipulate the adults to avoid or minimize accountability for their actions. Unfortunately, the Alternative Measures Program is not available to help these children. They fall through the *'gap'* until they commit a crime.

It is apparent to me, if we fill this *'gap'* before a crime has been committed, we can be most effective. To deal with these young people, several authorities are required to work together for the good of the child. Parents need to take responsibility and communicate openly with schools and Social Services to establish a partnership that supports the growth of the child. Schools and Social Services need to support each other. The child needs to fully understand how close he/she is to the criminal justice system. The criminal justice system needs to support the actions of the school and Social Services and the parent.

My plan to fill this gap is very simple, identify the major authority figures involved with the young offender, and identify what the young offender believes he has done, and provide immediate accountability and a process for restitution and redemption:

1. Initial contact or apprehension of the offender.
    a) Identify the authority figures involved with the youth.
    b) Release from custody a recommendation for Alternative Measures Program (if applicable.)
    c) Set up a meeting with the offender and his parental figures as quickly as possible.

2. Contact all the authorities identified at the time of the initial contact. Advise them of the meeting with the parent. Ask for background information from the authorities. Involvement i.e. School attendance, grades, discipline troubles, school teams. Social Services: reason for involvement, parental stability, potential family issues, addictions. Determine if there are other problems that need to be addressed. (This is very important because it opens the door for collaboration. Host the meeting with the parents and the offender. Separate the offender from the parents. Have the offender write out in detail what he or she did and describe the offence.
3. Have the offender identify and include what consequences they believe to be appropriate. Have the parent write out a brief family profile. (Get the parents to work together.)
4. Have the parents describe the details of the offence as they know them.
5. Have the parents set out their expectations of their child. This process needs to be done quickly. Allow 20 minutes maximum.
6. Separating the parent from the child is more important for the parents than the kids. It forces the parent to think about how involved they are in their child's life.
7. Reconvene the meeting
    a) Have the child present his/her report. Set out process ground rules to prevent interruptions.)
    b) Have the parents present their report. (Keep the parents on topic and not responding to the child's report.
8. Draft a Contract for Success.
    a) Set the contract out in four phases.
    b) State the conditions or standards desired by the school. I start with these conditions for three reasons.
        i. the school is usually not represented at the meeting.
        ii. writing out these requirements form an example for the next set of conditions.
        iii. these conditions are easily monitored.
9. State the conditions for conduct of the child at home. Establish these standards of conduct by first asking the child and then getting confirmation from the parents. This discussion often is the first time the child has been empowered to set rules for him/herself.
10. State the conditions for conduct of the parent in relation to the standards established for the child. Parents can become defensive

during this discussion. Keeping everyone focused on the present and the future conduct and expectations rather than the reflections on the past, is the biggest challenge at this point.
11. State the conditions of conduct required or expected by the police. The police are viewed as the last line of authority. Our role is to ensure compliance with the contract.

The following sample contract was drafted to address the problems created when a 12-year-old girl was caught skipping school and stealing cigarettes. The parents are Denise and Greg. Their daughter Ashley is the subject of the complaint.

Contract for Success

We agree to comply with the conditions set out in this contract.

1. Ashley agrees to:
    i) attend school.
    ii) achieve grades in school.
    iii) complete chores at home, including:
    iv) washing the evening dishes,
    v) cleaning the bathrooms once a week,
    vi) feeding the dog daily.
    vii) to stop smoking.
    viii) to comply with the check-in system (ask for permission to go out from Mom or Dad. Before leaving, provide the phone number, address and the name of a responsible adult at the location visiting. Phone home upon arrival at the location and return home on time.)
    ix) to call Constable Cole or his representative two times a week at the appointed times.
    x) to complete homework assigned by Constable Cole.
2. Denise and Greg agree:
    a) to stop smoking in the house.
    b) to get Ashley up and ready for school.
    c) to support the check-in system.
    d) to provide time just for Ashley to describe her day to us. We will listen and ask questions during this time.
3. Constable Cole agrees:
    a) to have his representative receive Ashley's phone calls.
    b) to check with all parties in this contract to ensure compliance.
    c) to find homework for Ashley. (Homework takes many forms, i.e. reading passages from the Bible or the Criminal Code, participating in various school and youth groups).

Signed:
Ashley _____
Denise _____
Greg _____
Constable Cole_____
Dated: _____

I have been using different strategies to improve the model for over three years. The model has evolved and has been adapted to fit different circumstances.

In the first year I ran the project entirely on my own. There were no volunteers. I took two phone calls a week from 34 different kids. By the end of the school year it was apparent I could not do everything myself.

I went into the schools and developed communication links for the kids with the school office staff and the principals. A very strong partnership developed, and my telephone load lessened. Unfortunately, my personal contact with each child lessened as well.

I explained my dilemma to a pastor friend of mine. He agreed to take some of the phone calls to help me out. I explained the nature of the contract and the reporting requirements. He worked with three kids successfully.

I started seeking out other volunteers to help with my kids. Experience has led me to believe volunteers can fulfil this part of the contract better than I can. Each volunteer is assigned one, to a maximum of three kids. Every two weeks, I meet with the volunteers as a group. The volunteers can contact me, almost immediately, should an emergency arise.

The model is successful for several reasons, including:

1. shared responsibility with the youth involved at every step in the process. The youth identifies the problem, establishes a code of conduct and holds other stakeholders in the contract accountable.
2. communication between all the parties involved with the youth is established.
3. the program starts almost immediately after apprehension.
4. the program provides continual contact with the police from the time of initial contact through to the conclusion of Alternative Measures consequence and into the future as required.

5. Challenges arose while implementing this model. They can be summarized under the following headings.
    i) number of youths brought into the program.
    ii) volunteers.
    iii) time management.
    iv) personalities.

Each of these challenges necessitated changes to the program. Initially the number of youths involved was very small. They came to my attention because I arrested them and subsequently recommended them to the Alternatives Measures Program. The numbers grew very quickly because of my direct involvement and partnership with the schools. Working on my own I reached the overload point very quickly.

This problem was addressed by sharing part of the process with volunteers, thus enabling more youth access to the support of the program.

Working with volunteers created its own challenges. A background check needs to be completed on each volunteer to ensure the safety of the children in the program. Volunteers need to be briefed on their roles and provided with copies of the contract. Volunteers need to keep notes and written records of their involvement with the youth. The very nature of the volunteer's role, having a conversation with a Young Offender, results in issues that are beyond the scope of the volunteer role. These issues range from child abuse and criminal activity to not understanding their schoolwork. The volunteer needs a reporting process and a supporting network. To this point I have provided both. I resolve most of the volunteer's issues by scheduling meetings with them every two weeks. I became the emergency on call person to support the volunteer when issues requiring immediate attention came to light.

The increase in the number of youths caused an increase in the number of volunteers. The more volunteers involved, the more time management became an issue. The program is being operated in and around my regular duties as a patrol constable. I utilize my unassigned time to support the volunteers. This worked well with three or four volunteers and the school support network, but the program has grown beyond my expectations and once again I am overloaded. Taking on more would affect both home life and patrol performance.

The natural next step for the growth of the program requires more police officers to be involved in it. More police officers supporting more volunteers could fill the gap for more first-time offenders.

Another possible next step could be the creation of a volunteer co-ordinator position. The co-ordinator could be a police officer or a civilian staff member. A police officer role would be defined as follows:

- identify all first-time offenders.
- conduct interviews and write contracts.
- contact schools.
- identify volunteers.
- support contract and volunteers.
- be the go to resource.

Non-police co-ordinator role could be defined as follows:

- identify all first-time offenders.
- identify the involved school.
- schedule the contract meeting for the police officer, parents and youth.
- assign the volunteer.
- schedule volunteer meetings.
- be the go to liaison between the volunteer and the police service.

The last issue that comes up from time to time is personality. Sometimes the volunteer and the youth don't like each other. Sometimes personal prejudices enter the picture. I address an issue of this nature by changing the volunteer. I ensure the new volunteer is aware of the previous issues and has a plan to accommodate the personality.

The program works because it has the flexibility to adapt to each individual situation while maintaining its original goal of filling the gap in the system. The result is a timely meaningful process involving the community, school, police, family and kids all working together.

One of my kids was charged with assault with a weapon and thus entered the court system. The assault was because of the kid bulling his peers at school. The school expelled the kid to a different school still in the city. The kid wrote his final exams in science yesterday. He got 98 per cent. He blamed his success on the mentor. The mentor use science as the means of communication with this kid.

The mentor is a grandma and she had the kid teach her his lessons. The kid has been in no trouble since my contact with him. The turnaround has taken just over a month.

My program is simple. I believe kids act out because they are not given other ways to express themselves. The program provides one-on one contact with a responsible adult role model. The mentor listens to the kid, provides positive feedback and introduces alternatives. All the adults or authority figures involved with the kid sit at a table and profile the kid. We establish what behaviours are unacceptable. Then we establish what the kid does do well.

We focus on the positive things and develop an action plan. Then we invite the kid into the meeting with his already developed plan for success. I have the kid present his plan to the group. As a unit we build on the kids plan to include the goals of the adult action plan. We write a contract for success and all parties sign it. The mentor is provided with the contract. The mentor frames his phone conversation with the kid around the contract. The contract provides open doors so that all parties working with the kid stay on the same page. The kid has achievable short and long-term goals and receives positive re-enforcement. The kid also has a clear understanding of what is expected and of the consequences. This provides an effective means for correction as required but more importantly a measuring stick for successes.

I am in the process of setting up a bulling program for the junior high-level schools. The plan is to present a 40 min lesson early in the next school year to most of my grade 7 students. The idea is to reinforce the lessons from the grade 6 DARE program and to set the ground rules right of the bat. The lesson will be followed up with the one on one attention of my program as required. We learned this year that a lot of kids simply don't know what bullying is. Our hope is to set the groundwork so that any future dealings with this issue will at least start with some basic knowledge.

Edmonton city councillors are considering a proposal put forward by the Edmonton Police Services that could see the city's public places bylaw amended to include harassment. Their plans are to ticket bullies who taunt, tease or otherwise harass their victims that could see bullies slapped with $250 fines. The existing bylaw covers several offences ranging from obstructing a public place without a permit to fighting in a public place.

Citizens Against Bullying Association of Northern Alberta

Citizens Against Bullying Association of Northern Alberta is a non-profit Society and Registered Charity comprised solely of volunteers. We have been in existence since June of 1999. We are dedicated to raising awareness about the problem of bullying behaviour amongst children. Current projects include:

Bi-monthly newsletter

A collection of bullying articles and information from around the world.

Website-Development and maintenance of A Canadian website with a chat room for kids and a discussion forum for families.

Online, children and their families can exchange information and share ideas. www.stopbullyingme.ab.ca

Bullying surveys

Part of our mandate is the collection of bullying statistics. CABA has developed a standard survey for use in schools who want to find out about bullying in their schools. Details available on website.

CABA works on several awareness programs at one time. Further awareness projects are awaiting funding.

Southeastern Alberta

Ray Van Schaick (Past District Governor of 37C) for Southeastern Alberta *says, "We are concerned that there has been no mention of a program that is in many schools across Canada knows as Lions-Quest. This is a program that's sponsored by Lions Clubs International and local clubs fund the training f teachers to use the program in individual schools. A major part of the program is just plain good citizenship. There is a segment of the program that deals with bullying and name-calling. Teachers tell us that the climate within the schools change greatly when this program is a part of the school curriculum. Those who are interested can contact a local Lions Club or Lions-Quest Canada at:* Unit 1 - 515 Dotzert Court, Waterloo, Ontario, N2L 6A7 800-265-2680

Innisfail Safe and Caring Community Association

The Innisfail Safe and Caring Community Association is supporting the Safe and Caring Schools curriculum by offering the five Toward a Safe and Caring Community Workshops to adults to encourage them to model and reinforce positive behaviour for all our children. Topics focus on the themes of respect, responsibility and cooperation, providing strategies to deal with: bullying, conflict, prejudice and anger.

Another initiative of the association is the Parent Child Mother Goose program offered to young parents and their babies/tots. It provides a bonding experience using interactive activities with rhymes and songs and an opportunity for parents to tell their own creative family stories. An important element provided by this program is to encourage the families about living *'in community'* and the support they can receive from each other.

Other projects supported by the association are the One Day Parenting Conference in October and the monthly Community partner meetings with other agencies and organizations at the Mary Morton Center on the 3rd Tuesday of each month. The ISACC is setting up an Anti-Bullying Column series in the local paper depicting bullying scenarios and asking community members to respond with solutions. Other weekly articles to encourage a viewpoint that *'all kids as our kids'* and *'it takes a village to raise a child'* are being supported by the local media.

Another project we are embarking on is a Bullying/Virtue Blitz of the local restaurant Waiting rooms. Tri-folds with information profiling a bullying act and the virtue to replace that bullying behaviour will be distributed to these locations.

For more information contact:

    Innisfail Safe and Caring Community Association
    Innisfail, Alberta T4G 1S9 Phone: (403) 227-0007

www.bullying.org is an award-winning web site that was created in Canada to help people around the world support each other in dealing with issues of bullying and teasing. http://www.bullying.org is a supportive international community where people can learn that they are NOT alone in being bullied and teased, that being bullied and teased is NOT their fault and that they CAN do something about it.

People can contribute their personal stories, poems, images, audio files, music and even animations and movies. It receives over 250,000 visitors from around the world every month and this number is growing steadily. It is a winner of the Childnet International Award that goes to projects that make the Internet a safer and better place for kids. It is also a finalist in the Stockholm Challenge Awards that recognize outstanding international projects that use information technologies make our world a better place in which to live.

Canadian Student must fix principal's teeth

A Regina high school student who punched his principal must do one hundred hours of community service and pay to get the man's teeth fixed. A $550 restitution order for dental work was part of a youth Court sentence imposed by Judge Leslie Halliday. He gave the youth a conditional discharge and put him on probation for a year.

Saying it appears the youth has an ongoing anger problem, Halliday directed him to follow any counselling recommended by his youth worker. He will also have to apologize to Yakichuk and the other students and teachers who witnessed the assault. *"It seems to me you were in a terrible rage that day... you were quite uncontrollable,"* Halliday said. Halliday said an assault of this nature on the main authority figure of a school is disturbing. A school is supposed to be a safe environment. The youth is required to stay away from Miller High School and Yakichuk, except for the purpose of making an apology.

The 17-year-old pleaded guilty last month to assaulting Miller High School principal **Bert Yakichuk** inside the school. Yakichuk met with the student on the day in question after learning he had skipped class. Yakichuk was punched in the face, kicked and pushed into a wall, which caused damage to his glasses and dental work.

In a victim impact statement, Yakichuk said he relives the assault when he walks down the hallway where the incident occurred.

How special schools can help with bullies and victims

Jer Doney said Grade 8 was hell for him. He was picked on regularly when he went to school. Doney used to be one of up to 3,000 students in Nanaimo-Ladysmith elementary schools who are bullies' prey. *"Guys used to come up to me and push me around and stuff."* He said. Being bullied was only one factor that led to Doney's poor attendance record at school.

Doney and *Newman* were both kicked out of their regular high school for causing problems and for being absent too many times. They now go to Five Acres alternate, a school with only 36 students. It's specially programmed to deal with and help kids who are bullies or have other problems. But not every child involved in an aggressor/victim situation can deal with their problems by going to a special school. And for parents of children being bullied every day in regular elementary schools, their lives can quickly turn to shambles. The school has tough rules on fighting, swearing and students earn credit for being good. Students follow the rules because they don't want to jeopardise their role at the school where they feel important and respected.

Jenn Newman said Five Acres helped her turn her negative, low self-esteem harsh attitude to making her a positive outgoing young lady with poise and confidence. **Jer Doney** who was picked on in regular schools, said it's the one-on-one relationship with counsellors and teachers at the school that helped him clean up his act.

Port Coquitlam, British Columbia

A Port Coquitlam school has taken the bluster out of bullies with a hard-nosed anti-bulling program. Students get an intensive six-week program on bullying. Parents report that their children are enjoying school instead of being unhappy and fearful. We get the whole community involved - the staff, the parents and the kids.

In Coquitlam, British Columbia, their **Bully B'ware's program called 'Take Action Against Bullying'** was written to educate students, parents, teachers and administrators. Its web page http://www.bullybeware.com covers:

- Act against bullying
- What is bullying?
- Common characteristics of bullying
- Kinds of bullies
- What makes a bully?
- What makes a victim?
- What happens to victims?
- Reasons why we must act against bullying
- Benefits of an anti-bullying policy
- What schools can do
- Students are key to a successful anti-bullying campaign.

They have a book, video and posters that help students, parents, teachers and administrators *'Take action against bullying.'*

Another British Columbia school listed bullying as being a big problem at their school. When one out of every four referrals to his office was bullying-linked, the principal of Kwayhquitlum Middle

School acted - forming a committee of parents, school staff and four students. What followed was months of consultation and information-gathering until they prepared a comprehensive bullying manual. The package identified various types of bullying, examines thinking of bullies, provides lesson plans for teachers, and includes surveys for parents and students to fill out.

Play about bullying

Jenny Young who is affiliated with **Electric Company,** a Vancouver-based troupe has had phenomenal success when presenting her one-woman performance *'The Shape of a Girl'* Canada-wide. Her play is about teen brutality and bullying. Her character is a 15-year-old girl who struggles with female violence and becomes obsessed with the Virk case. (**Reena Virk** was beaten and drowned by a group of teens in Victoria, B.C.). With such a topic, it's no wonder discussions after the play have been heated and emotional.

The response from the over 150 audiences is overwhelming. Most are amazed to discover that she's 25 - not 15 years old.

THE NETHERLANDS

School and Violence, causes and solutions

(Book by Bob van der Meer)

Dr. Bob van der Meer, a psychologist, is author of articles and books on students of not-Dutch origin, emancipation, violence, child abuse, motivation, bullying between students in schools, bullying between adults at work, problem solving, truancy, sexual harassment and leaving school without diploma. He can be reached at b.vandermeer@pesten.net

He was member of the board that carried out the nationwide research on violence in secondary education and on bullying in primary and secondary education; was member of the organisations for parents in education who initiated the Dutch action against bullying in education, titled *'Bullying, over and out.'* His book states:

Violence is a group problem, a societal problem and a problem of all centuries. The thesis in this book is that when one wants to end violence in schools adequately, three conditions are to be fulfilled. In the first place one must attack violence in a structural manner and not via one or more projects of short duration. In the second place it is advisable to dispose of an explanatory model of violence, in which model all possible and known causes of violence are included. And in the third place one should have knowledge about the psychological mechanisms or natural laws that are at hand when violence is at stake. These conditions are elaborated whereupon solutions are given.

Violence in schools is shown between pupils, pupils and teachers, teachers and pupils, between personnel, between school and parents and between parents and school. To stop violence in school, one should start with the shown physical, psychological and/or sexual violence, in other words bullying, between pupils. When this sort of violence is taken care of, the violence between the other groups should be resolved.

After that, one should take care of the direct violence of pupils against school (graffiti, demolishing or theft of school properties), the indirect violence of pupils against school (de-motivation problems, truancy, irregular attendance), the violence of pupils against society (graffiti, demolishing societal properties and criminality) and finally the violence of pupils against themselves (depression, auto-mutilation, and suicide).

The results of a pilot project in four multicultural schools in Utrecht along above-mentioned conditions are mentioned in chapter three, the last chapter of the book. To order book: http://www.pesten.net

Netherlands - Bullying at School: How to deal with it - **Vereniging voor Openbaar Onderwijs**

National Education Protocol against Bullying

The National Education Protocol against bullying aims to tackle the problem of bullying in children by a co-operative effort and so contribute to the happiness, well-being and the prospects for the future of children. The brochure entitled *'How to deal with bullying at school. Recommendations, consequences and detailed information'* was developed for a national campaign for tackling bullying in schools in a concrete way. The campaign that was started in 1994, proved to be a great success and the demand for information concerning ways to combat bullying grew. Based on the guidelines in this brochure, schools for primary and secondary education can develop a policy to put an end to the problem of bullying in such a way that all groups involved will be on the same wave-length, and will support one another, because co-operation is crucial to success. This co-operation can be made even stronger by signing the National Education Protocol against Bullying.

Parent associations, parents' councils, participation councils, school boards, management teams - everyone is responsible for ensuring that children are safe at school, so that they can develop to the best of their ability. By supporting each other and by creating a safe school environment, more pupils will enjoy going to school than is the case now.

Possible strategy

Seven Steps

1. The parents' council at the school submits this brochure to the competent authorities, the management team, the teaching staff, the participation council and, where appropriate, the pupils' council. After that, each group gives its opinion about the content of the brochure.
2. The comments on the brochure are collected by the competent authorities of the school. They are assessed, and a decision is made by the competent authorities about the approach to the problem of bullying that is to be taken at the school. All the groups within the school are informed of this decision.
3. All the groups/departments in the school undersign the protocol against building.
4. The parents' council/association sends a copy of the signed protocol to the relevant national organisation for parents in education.
5. All parents receive a copy of the protocol. Now of enrolling a new pupil, his/her parents also receive a copy of the protocol.
6. The poster (printed on the inside cover of this brochure) is put up in the school in a spot where it is clearly visible.
7. The competent authorities see to it that a plan is drawn up to implement the recommendations. This plan is submitted to all the groups / departments in the school. The concrete elaboration of the plan is incorporated in the school work plan, and thus constitutes an instruction that the activities mentioned for improving the *'safety'* among pupils be carried out.

Conditions and Recommendations

Bullying at school seems a complicated problem to tackle, but it is not as complicated as you might think. However, there are several conditions that must be met:

1. Bullying must be a **problem** by all parties: teachers, parents and pupils (those who are bullied, bullies as well as the silent majority).
2. The school must **prevent** the problem of bullying. A preventive approach consists, among other things, in raising the topic with the pupils, and subsequently laying down rules.
3. If, despite preventive measures, building crops up anyway, teachers must draw attention to it and take a **clear stand** against it.
4. Reject bullying in a clear way.
5. If, despite all the efforts to suppress it, bullying crops up again, the school must have a **direct (curative) approach** for dealing with it.
6. If a school or a teacher refuses to tackle the problem, or if this is done in the wrong way, or in such a way that it does not have any effect, then a **counsellor** needs to be called in. (At the request of the parent(s) of the child who is being bullied), this counsellor must submit a complaint to the Complaints Committee, which will investigate the problem and advise the competent authorities as to the measures that are to be taken.

These six conditions constitute the basis for six recommendations for tackling the problem of building at school.

Bullying: a problem

Recommendation 1

All five parties involved - the bully, the child who is being bullied, the rest of the class (silent majority), the teachers, and the parents - consider bullying to be a problem.

Consequences

By means of a seminar, all staff at the school is informed about:

- The difference between bullying and teasing;
- The extent of bullying among pupils;
- The parties and the psychological mechanisms that are involved in this kind of abuse of power
- The **five-track approach** to the problem consists of:

- Help for the child who is being bullied, in the form of advice and (in some cases) social skills training;
- Help for the build, in the form of social skills training or a course in coping with aggression;
- Help for the silent majority, which takes the form of mobilising this group;
- Help for the teacher, providing background information about the phenomenon, such as signs, causes, consequences and concrete (preventive and curative) ways of tackling it;
- Help for the parents, in the form of background information and advice.

Preventive approach

Recommendation 2

The school has developed a preventive approach to the problem of bullying.

Consequence: Teachers have been informed about ways of preventing bullying, have practised these techniques, and are able to apply them.

Drawing attention to the problem

Recommendation 3

If bullying crops up despite preventive measures, teachers must be able to draw attention to it.

Consequence: The teachers recognise the signs of bullying and practise ways of drawing attention to the problem.

Taking a clear stand

Recommendation 4

If teachers see that a child is being bullied, they take a clear stand.

Consequence: Taking a clear stand requires grasping the extent of the problem, knowing what the consequences are for the victim, but above all, being able to empathise.

Curative approach

Recommendation 5

The school has at its disposal several curative measures.

Consequences: Teachers are informed of the curative technique and develop their own skill in applying these through practice.

Recommendation 6

This recommendation fits only into the Dutch situation.

Advice to the parents of bullies

- Take the problem seriously.
- Don't panic: every child runs the risk of becoming a bully.
- Try to find out what the cause of the bullying might be.
- Make your child sensitive to what s/he is doing to others.
- Pay attention to your child.
- Stimulate your child to play sports.

Advice to the parents of children who are bullied

If the bullying does not happen at school, but on the street, you can ring the parents of the bully and carefully ask them to talk about it with their child. Use as your argument that every child must be safe on the street. Nobody can deny this.

Bullying at school can best be discussed with the teacher.

If your child has been bullied for a long time, this will call for a more extensive approach. Contact the teacher, visit the school to see what is happening there, together with your child, read books and watch videos about bullying. If your child will not let you talk to anyone about it, support your child, give it background information and make it clear to him/her that the school will tackle the problem with care. Before you make this promise, it is advisable that you ask the school if they do in fact handle this problem with care.

- Reward your child and help him/her regain his/her self-respect.
- Stimulate your child to practice a sport, so that he/she can excel in a game or a form of motor skill.
- If your child is being bullied at a sports club by his/her peers or classmates, ask the management to give the problem their attention and to it discuss with the children in the sense that each child must feel safe at the club.
- Keep the lines of communication open; keep talking to your child. Don't do this in a negative way but give advice as to how to put an end to the bullying. A negative way of asking, for example, is: "What did they do to you today?"
- Support your child in the belief that there will be an end to it.

- Have your child write down what it has experienced. This may well evoke emotional reactions in your child. This is all right, if the child is helped to work through its emotions and to express them.
- Let your child take part in social skills training that is provided by the RIAGG (regional institute for mental welfare) or the School Advisory Service. You should not allow your child to be excluded for the umpteenth time by sending it to an agency outside the school.
- Try to get the school to provide social skills training for all its pupils.
- Do not accept the situation. If the school will not cooperage, call in the help of the counsellor at the school to put an end to an unhealthy situation for your child.

Advice to all parents

- Take the problem seriously; it can also happen to your child
- Take the parents of the child who is being bullied seriously.
- Make the problem something that is shared by all.
- Ask for supervision on the playground.
- Talk to your child about school, about the way children relate to each other in the class-room, about what the teachers do, how they punish children. Occasionally ask them whether children are ever bullied.
- Provide information about bullying from time to time; who does it, what do they do, and why?
- Correct your child if it continually excludes others.
- Set a good example yourself.
- Teach your child to stand up for others.

Rob Limper - European Conference on Initiatives to Combat School Bullying: Keynote Addresses at the Goldsmith University, London

The Only Way to Combat Bullying is a Cooperation Between All Those Involved in School: Good Practice in the Netherlands Initiated by Parents. Van der Meei, a Dutch psychologist, gave the following definition of bullying:

"Bullying is a systematic, psychological, physical or sexual act of violence by a pupil or group of pupils with respect to one or more

classmates, who are not (any longer) in a position to defend themselves."

He also developed a method to deal with the problem. Several *conditions* must be met before one can effectively deal with the problem of bullying:

Essential conditions

1. Bullying must be seen to be a *problem* by all parties: teachers, parents and pupils (those who are bullied, bullies as well as the silent majority).
2. The school must act to *prevent* bullying. A preventive approach consists, among other things, in raising the topic with the pupils and their parents, and subsequently laying down rules.
3. If, despite preventive measures, bullying crops up anyway, teachers must draw attention to it and take an *unequivocal stand* against it.
4. Bullying must be *condemned* unequivocally.
5. If, despite all the efforts to suppress it, bullying crops up again, the school must have a *direct (curative) method* for dealing with it.
6. If a school or a teacher refuses to tackle the problem, or if this is done in the wrong way, or in such a way that it does not have any effect, then a *counsellor* needs to be called in. (At the request of the parent(s) of the child who is being bullied), this counsellor must submit a complaint to the Complaints Committee, which will investigate the problem and advise the competent authorities as to the measures that are to be taken.

In a seminar, inform all staff at the school about:

- The difference between teasing and bullying
- The extent of bullying among pupils
- The parties involved, and the psychological mechanisms that are at play in this form of abuse of power
- The five-track method to the problem

Five-track method

1. Help for the *child* who is being bullied, in the form of advice and (in some cases) social skills training
2. Help for the *bully*, in the form of social skills training or a course in coping with aggression
3. Help for the *silent majority*, which takes the form of mobilising this group

4. Help for the *teacher*, providing background information about the phenomenon, such as signs, causes, consequences and concrete (preventive and curative) ways of tackling it
5. Help for the *parents*, in the form of background information and advice

An effective way of keeping bullying within limits, stopping it, or preventing it altogether, is to lay down rules for the pupils. For children in primary years 1 to 4 (4-8-year-olds) this can be done by the teachers, and for primary years 5 to 8 (9-12-year-olds) and the first two years of secondary education, by the pupils themselves.

The recommendations, together with practical suggestions for possible activities and references to videos and books etc., were listed in a brochure that was published together with the National Education Protocol against Bullying.

The Bullying Test (PestTest)

The Bullying Test is a computer program with which pupils can indicate, anonymously, in the classroom, whether they are aware of bullying behaviour among their schoolmates. They are asked to indicate the extent to which this occurs, where it occurs, and when. They are also asked whether the teacher does anything about it, successfully or otherwise. The Bullying Test is intended for the pupils of the three highest classes in primary school and the first three years in secondary education. With this we have targeted the 9 to 15-year-old age group, the category in which bullying is most often seen.

Introducing the test in the classroom immediately raises the subject of bullying. It takes a pupil approximately three minutes to fill in the test. Then, it's the next pupil's turn. When all the pupils have done the test, it is a simple matter for the teacher to run up a final score. This test result can be discussed in the classroom in general terms. With that, the teacher knows where and when bullying occurs most frequently and he/she can take specific action. By running the test several times, a year bullying remains a topical subject, and the teacher can see whether the measures taken are having any effect, and whether the bullying occurs less frequently. So far, approximately 85% of the schools are using the Bullying Test.

Analysis

Bullying is now on the social agenda in the Netherlands. There is not a school in the country where the problem of bullying is not discussed. Parents have become more assertive. The theatrical performances are still being booked out. Parents' evenings are being organised. Several schools have put on musicals that deal with bullying. Each week we receive requests from pupils asking for material about bullying for school projects. Students ask us what possibilities are open to them for doing a work placement on bullying or writing a thesis. As soon as a broadcasting corporation decides they want to broadcast the subject again, they contact us. Press journalists present us with poignant cases and ask for a solution. Individual parents ring us and tell us about their victimised child, particularly when the school does nothing about it, or not enough in their opinion. These parents, or their children also ring Education Enquiries (a government telephone enquiry number) where bullying is currently a hot topic.

Why was this campaign such an overwhelming success?

1. Everybody can relate to the subject, the emotion, in some way and everybody understands what it means based on his/her own experience of school life.
2. The fact that bullying is a major social problem had been established beforehand based on scientific research.
3. Those directly involved, that is, the parents, through their (representative) organisations, acted on the grounds of the research results.
4. All parties in schools were involved in the campaign from the very beginning to create a broad base of support.
5. There was a specific method for dealing with the problem that was presented with concrete examples.
6. There was a symbol in the form of a protocol that people were asked to sign.
7. The attention of the media was attracted in a big way.
8. Repeatedly, new activities were added to the campaign by way of service to the schools.
9. The campaign is not short-term hype but is being deliberately sustained for several years, if possible for the duration of one primary school generation.
10. For the campaign, new products with which to reach the schools and the media are constantly being developed.
11. In the materials they were offered, and particularly in the approach to bullying, all parties recognised something that was to their own advantage. This had a motivating effect that was essential because only a concerted effort by all those involved can be effective in the fight against bullying.

CONCLUSION

School bullying must stop! This won't happen until society, education departments and the courts implement and enforce zero-tolerance policies relating to school bullying.

Our children are constantly exposed to violence - and our society needs to look seriously at cleaning up the violence we now witness in many of our sporting events. Children see grown men acting just like school bullies. And we wonder why they clone that behaviour! Sport used to be *'sportsmanlike'* but the violent actions we see during many of our sporting activities - can't be considered sportsmanlike at all.

Because bullies are driven by jealousy and envy, any child who is bright and popular is likely to be targeted by bullies. Parents, teachers and carers must ensure that these children are prepared to deal with bullying.

Children who are not bullies or victims have a powerful role to play in shaping the behaviour of other children. It's the 60 per cent of children within the school system who are not bullied or victimized who hold the key to stop bullying. Students who witness bullying have the potential to reduce bullying by refusing to watch bullying, reporting bullying incidents and/or distracting the bully.

Here are my recommendations that should result in a lower level of school bullying:

- Federal Education Departments of each country would set up and enforce anti-bullying school policies to ensure all students are protected consistently - no matter where they live in a country.
- Ensure that every school has an anti-bullying policy that is not only in place - but is enforced.
- Provide more involvement by community groups to counsel both targets and bullies to find out what is behind the bullying.
- More parental involvement with the schools via parent-teacher associations.
- More police influence in schools where required.
- Severe punishment or monetary fines for repeat offenders.
- Targets of bullying would be shown how to act more assertively.

- Targets need to have confidence that any reported bullying would be dealt with swiftly and effectively by authority figures.
- Children would be encouraged to speak up on behalf of children they see being bullied.
- Teachers would make it safe for their students to report any bullying incident by respecting the anonymity of the victim and witnesses.
- Bullies would know the consequences for bullying and schools would consistently enforce the rules.
- Bullies would obtain counselling, so they could learn how to behave in a socially acceptable manner.
- Until those issues are resolved, parents must be very selective in choosing their children's schools. They will avoid schools that lack anti-bullying policies and will be especially wary of staff that insist they have no bullying in their schools. It's these schools that have the worst bullying records. If the school does have an anti-bullying policy, make sure it's a good one that is not only effective - but is enforced. The key to a successful anti-bullying campaign is to involve everyone in the community so we need your help to make it happen!

BIBLIOGRAPHY

Kinchin, David, *Post Traumatic Stress Disorder – The Invisible Injury,* Success Unlimited, U.K. 2001.

Marr, Neil & Field, Tim, *Bullycide Death at playtime - An expose of child suicide caused by bullying,* Success Unlimited U.K. 2001

Field, Tim, *Bully in Sight - How to predict, resist, challenge and combat workplace bullying. Overcome the silence and denial.* Success Unlimited U.K. 2001

Fulton, David, *Supporting Children with Post-traumatic Stress Disorder: a practical guide for teachers and professionals,* David Fulton Publishers

Napier, M. & Wheat, K., *Recovering damages for psychiatric injury,* Blackstone Press

Wilkie, Dr. William, *Understanding Stress breakdown,* Millennium Books, 1995

Sutherland V. & Cooper, C., *Understanding Stress,* Chapman & Hall

Tedeschi, R. & Calhoun, L., *Trauma & Transformation; growing in the aftermath of suffering,* Sage, 1996

Vaknin, Sam, *Malignant Self-Love - Narcissism Revisited*

Cleckley, Hervey, *The Mask of Sanity,* CV Mosby Publishers, 1976

Samenow, Stanton E., *Straight Talk about Criminals and Inside the Criminal Mind*

Elliott, Michele, *501 ways to be a good parent,* Hodder & Stoughton, 1996 and

101 ways to deal with bullying: a guide for parents, Hodder and

Keeping safe, a practical guide to talking with children, Coronet Books, 1994, and

The Willow Street Kids: Be smart, stay safe, Pan Macmillan, and

The Willow Street Kids: Beat the bullies, Pan Macmillan, and

Bully Wise Guide, Hodder, 1999, and

Bullying: a practical guide for coping for schools, FT Prentice Hall, and

Female sexual abuse of children: the ultimate taboo, John Wiley

Elliott, Michele & Shenton, Gaby, *Bully Free,* Kidscape, 1999

Shenton, Gaby, *Beyond Bullying,* Kidscape, Bracher Giles & Martin, 1999

Evans, Patricia, *The verbally abusive relationship; how to recognize it and how to respond,* Adams

Seddon, Cindy & Lowrey, Cindy, *Take action against Bullying*

Kraizer, Sherryll, Ph.D., *The Safe Child Book*

Hare, Robert D., *Without Conscience, the disturbing world of psychopaths among us,* The Guilford Press, 1999 and
Work Rage (Narcissist Manager) Canada, and
The Magic of Believing, and
Getting Up When You're Down, and
Kiss Daddy Goodnight, Pocket Books, and
Making Peace With Your parents, Ballantyne Books NY
Dyer, Wayne, *You'll See it when you believe it,* Avon Books, and
Men Who Hate Women - The Women who Love them, Bantam Books, and
Toxic Parents, Bantam Books, and
Your Eroneous Zones, and
The Sky's the Limit, and
Smart Women - Foolish Choices, New American Library
Carnege, Dale, *Free From Fears,* Pocket Books, and
Snow White Syndrome, Jove Books, Berkley Pub. Group
Clout-Habel, Catherine, *Work Abuse – How to recognize it*, and
Work Abuse – How to recognize and survive it
Sullivan, Keith, *The Anti-Bullying Handbook,* Oxford University Press, 2000
Levy, Barrie, *Dating Violence: Young Women in Danger.*
Keller, Irene, *Benjamin Rabbit and the Stranger Danger*
Dyte, Kathy, *Play it Safe*
Girard, Linda, *Who is this stranger, and what should I do?*
Hechinger, Grace, *How to raise a Street-Smart Child*
Walker, Lenore, *The battered Woman*
Orion, Doreen, MD (stalking), *I know you really love me*
Ross, Dorothea M. Ph.D., *Childhood Bullying and teasing: what school personnel, other professionals, and parents can do*
Acaster, Desa, *Strategies for Developing Empathy in Children*
Crum, Thomas, *The Magic of Conflict,* Simon & Schuster, 1987
Drew, Naomi, *Learning Skills of Peacemaking,* Jalmar Press, California, 1987.
Roc, Kath & Hawke, Margaret, *Conflict Resolution,* Macmillan Education Australia, 1992.
Nelsen, Jane, *Positive Discipline,* Ballantine books 1987.
Duncan, Neil, *Sexual bullying: gender conflict and pupil culture in secondary schools,* Routledge, 1999
Pease, Alan, *Body Language - How to Read Others' Thoughts by their gestures,* Carmel Publications, 1981.

Olweus, D., ***Bullying at school: What we know and what we can do***. Oxford: Blackwell Publishers, 1993.

Sharp, S. & Smith, P., ***Tackling Bulling in Your School***, Routledge, London, 1994

Stones, Rosemary, ***Don't pick on me,*** Piccadilly Press, 1993

Romain, Trevor, ***Bullies are a pain in the brain,*** Free Spirit Publishing, 1997

Coloroso, Barbara, ***The Bully, The bullied and the Bystander***, Harper Collins

Field, Evelyn, ***Bully Busting,*** Finch, 1999

O'Donnell, Vivette, ***Bullying: a resource guide for parents and teachers***, Campaign Against Bullying, Attic Press, 1995

Brown, Sandra, ***Where there is evil***, Macmillan, 1998

Schaum, Melita & Parrish, Karen, ***Stalked: Breaking the Silence on the in America***, Simon & Schuster, 1995.

Kingsley, Jessica, ***New Perspectives on Bullying***

Rigby, Ken, ***Bullying in Schools and What to do about it***

Blase, Joseph & Blase, Jo, ***Breaking the silence: Overcoming the problem of principal mistreatment of teachers,*** Corwin Press, 2002

WEB CONNECTIONS

Tim Field (Success Unlimited - public speaking) Bully OnLine (web page) The Field Foundation
www.successunlimited.co.uk www.bullyonline.org
www.thefieldfoundation.org
UK The Andrea Adams trust www.andreaadamstrust.org
Mental Health Network www.mhnet.org/guide/trauma.htm
The Healing Centre Online www.healing-arts.org
Prolonged Adaption Stress Syndrome
 www.benzinger.org/pass.html
Canadian Traumatic Stress Network
 www.Play.psych.mun.ca/~dhart/trauma_net/index.html
Australian Trauma Web www.psy.uq.edu.au/PTSD
PTSD sites www.ptsd.com
Sam Vaknin, (narcississm)
 www.geocities.com/vaksam/index/htm
Anthony M. Benis (narcissism) www.Narcissm.homestead.com
Joanna Ashmun (narcissism) www.halcyon.com/jmashmun/npd
Lifeline www.lifelinemacarthur.org.au
Together we do better www.togetherwedobetter.vic.gov.au
Buddy Bear – The Alanah and Madeline Foundation
 www.buddybear.com.au jepcaa@internex.net.au
SOFWeb eduweb.vic.gov.au/bullying/index.htm
Bullying Everybody's Business
 www.kidshelp.com.au/info7/contents.htm
Reach Out! www.reachout.com.au
Mind Matters online.curriculum.edu.au mindmatters/index.htm
Judith Paphazy, Resilience Promotion jepcaa@internex.net.au
Peer Support Foundation Victoria psupport@peersupport.com.au
Stop Bullying! bevans@alphalink.com.au
West Education Centre: **Beat Bullying** wested@ozemail.com.au
Eliminating violence -Managing Anger www.ses.org.nz
No Bullying Starts Today luckyduck@dial.pipex.com
Police/Telecom "Stop Bullying" www.nobully.org.nz
Bullying Online (UK) www.bulying.co.uk
Scottish anti-bullying Network, Edinburgh abn@mhie.ac.uk
Anti-bully www.antibully.org.uk
UK Dept for Ed & Employment DfEE
 www.dfee.gov.uk/bullying/pages/home.html

The Wounded Child Project www.thewoundedchild.org
Selwyn College Anti-Harassment Team (New Zealand)
    www.aht-selwyn.school.nz
Dutch school bullying www.pesten.net
QIEU Bullying Policies www.qieu.asn.au
Bullying in USA www.bullypolice.org
Communities Against Violence Network www.cavnet.org
National Criminal Justice Reference Service www.ncjrs.org
Stalking Resource Center (SRC) www.ncvc.org/src/index.html
Anti-stalking web site www.antistalking.com
The Stalking Assistance Site www.stalkingassistance.com
Survivors of Stalking (SOS) www.soshelp.org
The Stalking Victims Sanctuary www.stalkingvictims.com
Victim Advocacy Program of the Capital District VACCD@aol.com
Victim-Assistance Online www.vaonline.org
Stalking FAQ www.state.ia.us/government/ag/stalker.htm
National Victim Centre www.ojp.usdoj.gov/ovc/help/stalk/info44.htm
Cyberstalking www.cyberangels.org/stalking
The Message Relay Center www.MessageRelayCenter.msn.com
Not Victims www.smalltime.com/notvictims
Harassment law UK www.harassment-law.co.uk
Beyond Bullying ww.cwpp.slp.pld.gov.au/bba/default.html
Beyond Bullying www.bulliesincorporated.co.nz
The Mobbing Encyclopaedia www.leymann.se/English/frame.html
National Union of Teachers www.teachers.org.uk
Northern Territory Work Health (2001) www.nt.gov.au/dib/wha
WorkCover Authority of New South Wales (2001)
    www.workcover.nsw.gov.au
WorkCover Corporation, South Australia (2001)
    www.workcover.com
Workplace Standards Tasmania (2001)
www.safetyline.wa.gov.au
New Perspectives on Bullying - Astam Books, Australia
    info@astambooks.com.au
UK National Work Stress Network www.workstress.net
Befrienders International (Suicide) wwwlbefrienders.org
Helene Richards and Sheila Freeman
    www.sheilafreemanconsulting.biz/bullying.htm
Canada safety Council
    www.safety-council.org/info/OSH/bullies.html
Australian Manufacturing Workers' Union www.amwu.asn.au

Symptoms of emotional abuse
www.lilaclane.com/relationships/emotional-abuse
Beating bullies in New Zealand www.bulliesincorporated.co.nz

South Australian Employee Ombudsman Gary Collis
www.employeeombudsman.sa.gov.au
www.oeo.sa.gov.au
Working Women's Centre S.A. www.wwc.org.au
Women's Executive Network - Canada
www.wxnetwork.com
Citizens Against Bulling Association (CABA) of Northern Alberta
Canada www.stopbullyingme.ab.ca caba@stopbullyingme.ab.ca
Dr. Arnold Nerenberg - Road rage www.roadrage.com
Workplace Services SA www.eric.sa.gov.au
Equal Opportunity SA www.eoc.sa.gov.au
Industrial Court SA www.industrialcourt.sa.gov.au
Acts and regulations SA
www.parliament.sa.gov.au/dbsearch/legsearch.htm
Spanish Website www.psicoter.es
The Canadian Safe School Network
www.cssn.org/pages/home.htm
The Workers Health Centre ACT www.workershealth.com.au
admin@workershealth.com.au
ACTU *"Work on Life"* e-bulletin www.actu.asn.au
Australian Services Union - workplace bullying
asuclerical-nsw.asn.au/campaigns/w.html
International Labour Organization, Geneva www.ilo.org
New Zealand Council of Trade Unions union.org.nz
UnionSafe, NSW unionsafe.labor.net.au

www.ingramcontent.com/pod-product-compliance
Lightning Source LLC
LaVergne TN
LVHW051553070426
835507LV00021B/2565